The Fire of God

John Michael Talbot

The Fire of God

TROUBADOUR FOR THE LORD

1993
Troubadour for the Lord
RR 3, Box 608, Eureka Springs, AR 72632

Printed in the United States of America.

Contents

Introduction

It is time for a new revolution! Never before in the history of the human race have we faced such demanding and grave issues. And never before have we had such profound potential to affect the whole of the human race for good. The nuclear arms race, social injustice, and rampart poverty threaten a world that is potentially more capable of meeting people's needs than ever before.

As I travel around the country and the world, I sense that people are ready for a revolution. Not a revolution of military power and political intrigue, but one bearing the mark of the gospel of Jesus Christ. It is a spiritual revolution—one guided by the Holy Spirit and presided over by God the Father. It is a revolution that can shake the nations of the world by converting the human heart. It is the establishment of a nation of God that transcends all earthly nations and can unite them all in the sharing of divine and human love.

But you cannot share what you do not possess. You cannot bring a revolution if you have not first been revolutionized. You cannot evangelize unless you have first been evangelized. You cannot bring justice unless you have first been justified. You cannot bring peace unless you first know inner peace. You cannot give the gift of salvation unless you have been saved. All of this is only possible in Christ.

This desire for a gentle revolution is like a divine fire that burns on the face of the earth. Jesus says, "I have come to set a fire on the earth. How I wish it were ablaze already!" But this fire must inflame human hearts before it burns openly in the world. It must burn away all that is not of God from our personal life and lifestyle before our nations and cultures can change. It must purify us individually and make us morally strong. It must burn like an ember of love within our hearts to make us sensitive and kind. People must change before nations can change.

Recent polls show that the preoccupation and obsession of our Western world is money. We are the most materialistic nation ever to exist on the face of the earth. We have more than anyone has ever had. We are warmer in the winter, cooler in the summer, gluttonously fed with delicious foods, better housed, and our lives are medically prolonged. No culture has ever before experienced such material blessings.

Yet our blessings are the curse of the world. Our wealth creates the poverty of the world. We are a minority of the world's population hoarding a vast majority of the world's goods. For every luxury we enjoy, some innocent victim is deprived of his basic need. The success of the rich enforces the failure of the poor. The blessing we so lustfully pursue forces a curse and denial of those who seek only basic survival. Even our Western Christianity propagates the false gospel of prosperity rather than the gospel of Jesus Christ. Our consumer-oriented media propagate a sugar-coated gospel that subliminally brainwashes us into believing it is God's will for us to live in this "prosperity." Our preachers live like rich young rulers, and our gospel singers parade around like the kings and queens of secular rock. Our gospel has been secularized by the way people preach and propagate the holy.

We must follow in the footsteps of the real Jesus if we are to be real Christians. Our life-style must be conformed to the life of Christ. Did Jesus live in such materialistic indulgence? The answer is an obvious and unequivocable "no." We must distinguish between our wants and our needs, for our wants are killing the needy of this world! We must join in the life of the Jesus who walked this earth in poverty so that others might know the Bread of Life. In Christ, our life itself must become the bread for the hungry world and God's wealth for the poor.

I have been able to rise to this challenge myself only by meditating on God as a fire and allowing Him to inflame my whole life. This means allowing the fire of the Spirit to burn away all that is not of God from my feelings, my thoughts, and my life-style. It means allowing Him to inflame my soul to its very marrow so that my life might be positively strengthened and transformed. It means allowing this flame to become like a burning ember in my heart that both purges and warms my whole life throughout all my days.

Only the fire of God can eliminate and replace the fire of materialism, first in our hearts and lives and then in the world. It is also the only antidote to other selfish fires that blind us and lead us away from "the way, the truth, and the life." These other destructive fires have to do with lust, anger, and the tongue. And all of them, if left unextinguished, can fan themselves into the communal fire of a nuclear holocaust, for each is a mini-holocaust capable of destroying the individual soul, and the cumulative effect has staggering, universal repercussions.

The fire of lust blocks the free-moving power of the Holy Spirit in our lives. Anger burns within the human heart with a power strong enough to destroy every decent idea, action, and relationship. Sins of the tongue—negativity, gossip, lies—spread like wildfire through families, communities, and nations. We cannot expect to reverence life when we do not revere the Word of life that spoke all living things into existence. We cannot expect to influence for good the destructive and oppressive powers of the world when we continue to fan the flames of sin in our souls. We must first let the healing fire of God burn away our private sins before we can expect His power to change the public problems facing our world.

This book is a meditation and study on the fires of sin and on the healing fire of God. It is a look at the analogy of both God and sin as either a destructive or constructive fire, as seen in scripture, in mystical tradition and in the teachings of the Church. As a Franciscan I cannot help but also emphasize the use of this fire image by St. Francis and St. Bonaventure.

It is my prayer that this book will help to inspire both me and my readers in a way similar to the fire that burned within St. Francis in his radical imitation of the life and gospel of Christ. Lenin once said that if there were only ten St. Francises in the whole world, there would be no need for what became the Communist revolution. I pray we can rise to meet both the challenge and the threat of communism, the nuclear arms race, and global poverty by radically living the gospel of Jesus Christ after the manner of St. Francis today. If we allow the fire of the gospel to burn within our souls, then we will succeed. Otherwise, both we of the Church and the people of the world will grow spiritually cold.

If the fire of God explodes within our deepest soul, then the fire of a nuclear holocaust can be deterred. No policy, no treaty, no peace pastoral will ever deter this atrocity. Only the fire of God exploding within individual human hearts can keep this nuclear fire from exploding across the face of the earth.

If the fire of God warms the human heart, then it will dispel the cold of human sins. It will feed the hungry, clothe the naked, bring release to the prisoners, and redress the wronged. Most importantly, it will rekindle the love of our divine Savior within us personally and save a multitude of eternal human souls. Only the fire of God can redeem all nations and all political systems, for it first redeems living people. It rights all wrongs, for it lights all hearts. Once hearts change, then people change; and once people change, then the nations of the world will change. The structures that oppress are transformed into structures that liberate only when human hearts are set free by God's love!

This love is a fire, a living flame of love! To dispel the coldness within our hearts and the sin in the world, let us now look to the righteousness and love of the fire of God.

1
The Fire of the Holy Spirit and Purgation

For the Christian, the fire of the Holy Spirit is the most frequently remembered image of the fire of God. The fire of the Holy Spirit is promised as early as John the Baptist and is finally experienced at Pentecost. Since that time it has been the work of the Holy Spirit which has kept the fire of God alive in every believer's heart.

John the Baptist says, "I baptize you in water for the sake of reform, but the one who will follow me is more powerful than I. I am not even fit to carry his sandals. He it is, who will baptize you in the Holy Spirit and fire. His winnowing fan is in his hand. He will clear the threshing floor and gather his grain into the barn, but the chaff he will burn in unquenchable fire."

The Acts of the Apostles describes the day of Pentecost: "When the day of Pentecost came, it found them gathered in one place. Suddenly from up in the sky there came a noise like a strong, driving wind which was heard all through the house where they were seated. Tongues as of fire appeared, which parted and came to rest on each of them. All were filled with the Holy Spirit. They began to express themselves in foreign tongues and make bold proclamations as the Spirit prompted them."

Here the fire of the Spirit is given as a constant. It is our life-style that reacts differently to its presence. For some it will be punishment, for others comfort. For some it will purge, for others it will strengthen. For some it will be hell, for others it will be heavenly. For all it will test and purge, even if in the end it will make us strong.

John of the Cross says, "This flame of love is the Spirit of its Bridegroom, which is the Holy Spirit. . . . This is the language and these the words God speaks in souls that are purged, cleansed, and all rekindled. . . . When the soul is in the state of spiritual purga-

1

tion...this flame of God is not so friendly...the Holy Spirit wounds it by destroying and consuming the imperfections of its bad habits.... The very fire of love which afterwards is united with the soul, glorifying it, is that which previously assails it by purging it.... This flame of itself is extremely loving, and the will of itself is excessively dry and hard.... Hence the very flame that is now gentle, since it has entered within the soul, is that which was formerly oppressive, assailing it from without."

The call of Isaiah begins with his having a vision of angelic worship in the heavenly temple. All is holy and filled with glory so that "the house was filled with smoke." Isaiah says, "Woe is me, I am doomed! For I am a man of unclean lips, living among people of unclean lips; yet my eyes have seen the King, the Lord of hosts!" Isaiah is afraid for he knows that "no man can see the face of God and live." The story continues: "Then one of the seraphim flew to me, holding an ember which he had taken with tongs from the altar. He touched my mouth with it. 'See,' he said, 'now that this has touched your lips, your wickedness is removed, your sin purged.'"

Here the fire of God is a purging fire, used to make us holy and strong. Isaiah speaks of the process of taking unrighteousness and turning it into righteousness by fire: "How has she turned adulterous, the faithful city, so upright! Justice used to lodge within her, but now, murderers. Your silver is turned to dross, your wine mixed with water. Your princes are rebels and comrades of thieves; each one of them loves a bribe and looks for gifts. The fatherless they defend not, and the widows plea does not reach them.... I will turn my hand against you, and refine your dross in the furnace, removing all your alloy. I will restore your judges as at first, and your counselors as in the beginning; after that you shall be called city of justice, faithful city."

It is the coming of the fire of the Spirit that purges our life in an instant. It is like a hot blast that powerfully burns away all the chaff of our life. After receiving this divine fire we begin to speak and act differently. The foul language and coarse jesting that used

2

to proceed from our lips no longer seem necessary. The selfish behavior and unjust judgments no longer seem fair. Suddenly, in an instant, our life is changed. Our sin is purged by this fire of God and all that is left is a genuine desire for righteousness!

St. Paul also speaks of the fire of God as a purging fire. He says, "No one can lay a foundation other than the one that has been laid, namely Jesus Christ. If different ones build on this foundation with gold, silver, precious stones, wood, hay, or straw, the work of each will be made clear. The day will disclose it. That day will make its appearance with fire, and fire will test the quality of each man's work." Paul is speaking specifically of a purging after death and at the second coming of Christ, but the general principle of a test or purge of fire applies all during life. As St. Peter says, "Do not be surprised, beloved, that a trial by fire is occurring in your midst. It is a test for you, but it should not catch you off guard." As he states earlier in his first epistle, he is referring primarily to trials of suffering in this life. But in light of John the Baptist's reference to the fire of God in connection with the Spirit, and the outpouring of the Spirit spoken of as "tongues of fire" in the Acts of the Apostles, it is appropriate to see this fire as the Holy Spirit.

But fire is also used to describe specific sins such as materialism, anger, and lust that need to be purged from our lives. In this sense, we use fire to fight fire. The fire of sin can be fought only with a fire of God that burns even stronger within the soul.

It is almost as if the fire itself is passive. It will be used either for good or for evil, but it will burn one way or the other. It can either be the fire of sin or the fire of God. One is a fire that destroys, the other is a fire that saves. Likewise, it can either be the fire of God's punishment or God's love. Even within God's love there is a chastisement for loving correction and there is the pure flame of God's presence and love. All of these are spoken of in scripture. One thing is certain: fire will burn in our life; it is up to us to choose which kind of fire it will be—the fire of sin or the fire of God.

2
The Fire of Materialism

We live in a frightening time. Never before has the world enjoyed such material blessings from God, yet never before has poverty been so widespread. Never before has the world produced so much food, yet most of the world still goes to bed hungry. Never before have we known such medical advancement, yet disease is still rampant. Never before have we been so able to bring prosperity and life to so many, yet this very year millions will die of starvation and disease. In today's world the rich keep getting richer, but the poor remain desperately poor.

We Christians of the West must realize that we are not just part of the problem, we *are* the problem. We, the people of a Western culture, are a minority of the world's population, yet we possess a majority of the world's goods. Yes, we produce a good portion of those goods, but we do not sufficiently share them with others. We often make use of the cheap labor of the Third World to produce our successful products, but we do not share that success with the very laborers who helped us produce these goods so successfully and so cheaply.

St. James speaks of this disproportion when he says, "See what you have stored up for yourselves against the last days. Here, crying aloud, are the wages you withheld from the farmhands who harvested your fields. The cries of the harvesters have reached the ears of the Lord of hosts. You lived in wanton luxury on the earth; you fattened yourselves for the day of slaughter. You condemned, even killed, the just man; he does not resist you. As for you, you rich, weep and wail over your impending miseries. Your wealth has rotted, your fine wardrobe has grown moth-eaten, your gold and silver have corroded, and their corrosion shall be a testimony against you; it will devour your flesh like fire."

This is very similar to St. James's approach to sin in general. Of sin he says, "Once passion has conceived, it gives birth to sin, and when sin reaches maturity it begets death." For St. James, materialism is a sin that brings forth a fire of death. It kills the poor. It eventually even kills the rich.

The words of James are inspired directly by the words of Jesus Christ. Jesus says, "Do not lay up for yourselves an earthly treasure. Moths and rust corrode; thieves break in and steal. Make it your practice instead to store up heavenly treasure, which neither moths nor rust corrode nor thieves break in and steal. Remember, where your treasure is, there your heart is also."

Jesus makes no bones about it. His words are frightfully clear. He says, "You cannot give yourself to God and money. . . . No man can serve two masters. He will either hate one and love the other or be attentive to one and despise the other." When Jesus sends His apostles out to evangelize, He cuts to the heart of the possibility of materialistic motives or gain. He says, "Provide yourselves with neither gold nor silver nor copper for your belts; no traveling bag, no change of shirt, no sandals, no walking staff. The workman, after all, is worth his keep." He says to us all, "None of you can be my disciple if he does not renounce all his possessions." The words are simple. The words are clear.

He is aware that this instruction not only brings us inner freedom, but also provides for the needs of the poor. Luke's gospel says, "Sell what you have and give alms. Get purses for yourselves that do not wear out, a never failing treasure with the Lord which no thief comes near nor any moth destroys." Of course, in the story of the rich young ruler, Jesus says, "If you seek perfection, go, sell all your possessions, and give to the poor. You will then have treasure in heaven. Afterward, come back and follow me."

This gospel brings good news to the poor. It evens out the distribution of wealth and brings a godly equality to all human beings created in the image of God. As St. Paul says, "There should be a certain equality. Your plenty at the present time should supply their need so that their surplus may one day supply your need, with equality as the result."

And lest we limit our charity to other Christians, or to those who can repay us in some way, Jesus says, "Love your enemies, do good to those who hate you. . . . Give to all who beg from you. . . . If you lend to those from whom you expect repayment, what merit is there in it for you? Even sinners lend to sinners expecting to be repaid in full. Love your enemy and do good; lend without expecting repayment. . . . This will prove that you are sons of your heavenly Father, for his sun rises on the bad and the good, he rains on the just and the unjust. . . . You must be perfect as your heavenly Father is perfect."

Jesus equates the poor with Himself, and tells us that we ourselves will be judged according to how we love Him in this world's poor. "I was hungry . . . I was thirsty . . . I was a stranger . . . naked . . . ill . . . in prison. . . . I assure you as often as you did it for one of my least brothers, you did it for me. . . . As often as you neglected to do it to one of these least ones, you neglected to do it to me."

There are, of course, theological rationalizations to lessen the challenge and the bite of Jesus' words. We can emphasize poverty of spirit rather than material poverty. We can point out that Jesus had wealthy friends, or that He Himself associated freely with the rich as well as with the poor. But none of this would spur us on to action. We need to let Jesus' words make us uncomfortable. We need to squirm a bit. Then, perhaps, we will really seek God in prayer. Then the Holy Spirit Himself will tell us what to do about our own possessions.

Now is the time for action! It is no longer enough to just give a little bit of our money in the yearly collection for relief. We must change our life-styles. It is the American life-style that oppresses the poor of the Third World. We must differentiate between our wants and our needs, for our wants are killing the needy! If we live according to our needs rather than according to our wants, we will meet the needs of all. Otherwise the poverty and the killing will continue. The result of this poverty is death. And it kills *real people.*

My Experience

Let me tell you about the poverty I have seen. I visited Port-Au-Prince, Haiti, to see the worst slums in the Western Hemisphere. These slums are, ironically, called Boston and Brooklyn. I had never seen poverty like this—twenty-five people living in a twelve-by-twelve-foot hut made of corrugated tin and twigs, or leftover lumber. The heat in the huts gets up to about 120 degrees during the day. Between every five or so huts runs a ditch in which flows water mixed with sewage and garbage. The children play in these ditches and sometimes stop to drink from them. Obviously, many children die of parasites and disease. Infant mortality is high. The government did not allow the missionaries to put in a proper water system. They seemed to like to keep their people poor.

Haiti is only one example among many. It is a country just off the coast of the United States. The United States is the richest country in the world, yet Haiti is the poorest in the whole Western Hemisphere. For years we supported their dictators in the name of defending capitalism, and we turned their "boat people" away from our abundant shores. Those who would not turn back to Haiti died in the rough ocean waters. Those who remained in Haiti died in poverty.

At the time of my visit, Haiti suffered from 80 percent unemployment. The average per-capita income was barely $100 a year. The land had been deforested early in this century; so the topsoil had washed out to the sea under the heavy rains. Haiti's farmland is gone.

There is a little outside industry from Korea and the United States. This provides some jobs, but these border on slave labor as working conditions rival the children's workhouses of our own country at the turn of this century. There simply aren't many jobs. Haiti remains desperately poor.

Even with the best success at calling in outside help, it will be fifty years until this land is on its own two feet. Experts in soil redevelopment have been called in, but their work takes time. Until

8

they succeed, the people of Haiti need outside help. Without our help they will die.

On the positive side, our Franciscan Mercy Corps, a world relief organization, is doing something in northern Ethiopia and the Sudan, among other places. In northern Ethiopia the people are starving. The north is made up of Coptic Christians. The official government of Ethiopia is Communist. The Christians do not support the Communist government; so the government decided to cut off most of the relief to the north. During the much-publicized drought in Ethiopia, the need ratio north to south was about forty to one. The actual distribution ratio south to north was . . . guess what? About one to forty! This means the distribution of aid to the Ethiopian drought victims was exactly opposite to the actual needs.

To meet this need we began smuggling relief to our brothers and sisters in the north through the Sudan. We could not get to them through the front door, so we got in through the back door. Sometimes "it is better to obey God than to obey men." This was one of those times.

With the help of a grant from the U.S. Government we began trucking "rehydration units" to the people of the north by night. We could not do so during the day because MIG fighters patrol the roads by air and attack any unauthorized caravans. Some have actually been attacked and destroyed!

These rehydration units amount to packets of water and basic vitamins designed to keep a human being alive for a few days. It isn't much, but it does save precious human lives and buy us a little more time. We have also sent in water-development teams to drill deep wells into the desert to find the hidden reservoirs of water far below. It is still too early to see any long-term results. We must help with a Band-Aid or these people will die!

Then there is the Sudan. Up until now it has been the Franciscan Mercy Corps' stable base of operations. But the drought is shifting. It will hit Sudan about the time this book is published. The experts project that some five million people will die in the Sudan in one year!

Sudan also has about one million refugees a year coming in from its war-torn neighbors of Ethiopia and Chad, one to either side. Many of these people need medical assistance. Along with the mounting needs of the native Sudanese, crisis in the Sudan is intense.

The Sudanese Government has alloted a good portion of its budget to meet the medical needs of these people, but the currency of Sudan is virtually worthless on the world market. They can allot all they want, but they can't actually buy anything. The Franciscan Mercy Corps is trying to give medical assistance in the Sudan.

Or there is Honduras: here the Mercy Corps goes in to live among the people of the back villages of the jungle. We send in qualified missionary families to live a life of poverty with the poor. The most important ministry is simply to be present with them and to show them that you care. But there are physical needs. They are so great that some of the solutions are very simple. Because the people's diet consists mainly of beans and rice, one of the greatest things we can do is simply teach them to grow their own vegetables. A person who knows even the basics of hygiene becomes a valuable expert. It takes only a little to help these precious people a lot.

One could go on and on, country after country, crisis after crisis. Poverty is real. It covers most of this planet we call Earth. It kills.

There are many valid and good relief agencies doing what they can to help the poor and the dying. The Franciscan Mercy Corps is only one of them. But it is not enough just to give money to a relief agency. We must change our lives. The Mercy Corps is not looking for a mailing list from which to solicit impersonal donations. We are looking for a *corps*, an army of people dedicated to helping the poor by totally embracing the gospel of Jesus Christ as a way of life. We don't just need money, we need changed lives.

Affluence or Materialism

Affluence is a sign of health. Materialism kills. It is good to have our basic needs met by God's grace and then to permit the overflow from our abundance to meet the needs of others. This is godly affluence. It is bad, however, to keep more than we need in order to satisfy our every want, thus blocking the flow of abundance to meet the basic needs of the poor. Materialism blocks the flow of charity and love.

Godly affluence is like a cup that is filled with living water and overflows to people dying of thirst in the parched desert. Materialism does not allow the water to overflow. It wants the water only for itself. So it builds the sides of the cup higher and higher. Soon it no longer resembles a cup. It looks first like a glass, then like a pitcher or a Thermos bottle. Finally it builds up its walls so high it no longer looks like anything that would hold living water. It looks more like a missile silo!

I once sat next to a well-known economist on an airplane. He was on his way to give a talk in Los Angeles. We began talking about the fair distribution of the world's wealth in accordance with the teachings of the Church. I asked him if our materialism really contributes to the poverty of the Third World, or does our prosperity actually help raise the living standard of the world?

He said that in the beginning the prosperity of one culture or nation actually does help do away with the poverty of another. It pulls the standards of the world up. It provides jobs and economic growth for all. But, he said, there is an undefinable line that, once crossed over by a few, actually pushes the many back down. I asked him if we had crossed over that line as a nation. He laughed and reached his hand high into the air to demonstrate just how far over the line we had crossed! He said that without question the prosperity of our nation actually causes the poverty of the poor.

Again, we are a minority of the world's population hoarding a vast majority of the world's wealth. What we have to satisfy our wants takes from the world's resources which could be used to meet the needs of others. We must distinguish between our wants and our needs, for our wants are killing the needy. I cannot say it enough!

We must change our life-styles, for the life-style of the few is depriving the many of basic necessities. Where there is poverty, there is rebellion against the government. Where there is revolution, there is war. Where there is war, nuclear holocaust becomes an ever-present possibility. If we want to do away with rebellion, war, and the possibility of a nuclear holocaust, we must do away with poverty.

If we want to defend the free-enterprise system we should freely divest ourselves of some of our capitalistic wealth. If we want to fight the very real threat of communism, we had best freely distribute our many goods among this world's many poor. Otherwise an atheistic communism might overtake us in a way that does not recognize our God-given freedom of choice.

Discipline as the First Step to Freedom

When we first begin to give up our wants, it will seem difficult indeed. Our wants and habits will kick and scream when they are deprived of their usual allotment of luxury. They will tell us they will surely die without it. But it is a lie. Do not believe them. After a while they will begin to settle down and behave, and you will be able to tell what your needs really are. You will find out how little you really need in order to survive.

It is much like fasting. When you first deprive your body of food, your body tells you it is dying of hunger. But this is not true. Your body is just accustomed to the luxury of eating. After your body quiets down, you find out that you really feel quite good. In fact you have more energy then you've had in years. Your mind is clear and your reflexes sharp. Only after a period of time will your body really need food again. Of course you cannot fast for weeks at a time frequently. But once or twice a year it is actually healthy to "deprive" the body of food through a Godly fast.

The same thing holds true to giving up material possessions. When you first think about giving up the things you want but do not really need, you will think that survival without them will be unbearable. Life would be boring. What would you do with your spare time without "things"? But once you give them up you find out just how little you really needed them. And in addition you find more time for the prayer you never seemed to have time for before.

I am reminded of St. Francis of Assisi. When he first reached out to embrace the leper, he felt sick to his stomach. The sight of lepers had always nauseated him. How could he possibly reach out to embrace them? Yet God told him to do so! In obedience he forced himself to do so. Guess what happened? As soon as he actually embraced the poor leper, his nausea went away.

When Francis first lived with the beggars he looked down into the contents of his own beggar's bowl with disgust. Yet in order to minister to the beggars he had first to live as one. He reached to share the beggar's meal in blind obedience to God. As soon as he actually ate this feast of garbage, it became for him a sweet and heavenly banquet of God's grace. What was once bitter was made sweet through the love of Jesus Christ for the poor.

We can do so much more than we think possible! If we break free of the yoke of our cultural materialism we will discover a newfound personal freedom to fly unto the heights of heaven in Christ.

I am reminded of a famous doctor in Canada. Even with socialized medicine he made a lot of money. He and his family lived very well. He was a wealthy and successful man. Then, in obedience to the call of Jesus Christ, he and his wife made a covenant with God's poor. They gave up their palatial home and moved into a rental home in the city. They gave away all the money they made except for what they needed to live on for one week! They have several children of their own but have adopted many others.

They donate one day a week to organize many other people to give a sack of rice and beans to send to the poorest of the poor in Calcutta.

This couple broke free of their Western materialism to discover an exciting new way of life in Jesus Christ. They have all of their needs met, but they do not satisfy all their wants. Yet the more they deprive themselves of their physical wants, the more they find their spiritual needs satisfied abundantly in Christ and in service to Christ's poor. I visited this man and his wife and truly felt I was in the presence of two living saints.

"Unholyland Tours"

I also recommend to you what has recently been dubbed "unholyland tours." Most Americans spend a lot on travel and vacations. Many save up a long time to travel to the Holy Land where Jesus actually walked.

I recommend spending some of that money to walk where He walks *today*. Spend some of that money to visit an impoverished nation of the Third World. You say it is enough to visit our own inner cities. True, the poverty there is bad. We have problems of our own. But you have never seen poverty until you have looked upon the slums of "Boston" or "Brooklyn" in Port-Au-Prince, Haiti. It is not enough to see it on television. You must smell it. You must feel the dirt of it between your toes. You must experience it. I guarantee that once you have experienced it, your life will never be the same. You will never be able to eat well without remembering those who starve. You will never be able to sleep in comfort without remembering those with no place to rest their heads. You will never be able to get medical treatment without remembering those who get none.

To experience poverty of this sort makes all of our feeble questions about "helping only those who help themselves" and the like seem suddenly unimportant. All that is important now is saving one human life for just one more day. Each day is a lifetime. Jesus gave His life to save theirs. Shouldn't we do the same?

A Caring Heart

Consider the spirituality of Mother Teresa of Calcutta. Many people criticize her for not solving the root problem of poverty. Her Sisters can help only a handful of the poor when compared to the enormity of the problem. She responds by emphasizing the importance of one human soul in God's eyes. This is the soul God Himself created in His image. It is the soul He sent Jesus to die on the cross for. It is the soul all the angels in heaven rejoice over when he or she turns to the saving love of God. In this sense Mother Teresa gets to the source of the problem better than any development agency that deals only with numbers and externals. Mother Teresa reestablishes the priceless value of each individual human soul. If we could all walk with this appreciation we would soon do away with the widespread poverty that inflicts most of our world. We would suddenly begin to care.

This, too, is the key to our presence among the poor. More important than any efficient program is our presence among them to care. We can bring them programs without love, and they will hate us. We can bring them love, and almost any legitimate program will work. To look them in the eye and care for their life; to smile back into the expectant faces of the children; to take the time simply to care as one child of God for another: these are the things that make our presence among the poor helpful in the eyes of God.

I would like to relate the story of a Franciscan Mercy Corps couple who visited one of our mission families in Honduras. During their stay with the family, the Franciscan couple asked to visit the Catholic church. They were taken to a little building that looked more like a shack than one of our American or European edifices.

15

Inside, the congregation had gathered to sing while they waited for the monthly visit of the missionary priest. As soon as these two visitors walked through the door, every eye turned to them, thinking the man in the simple garb was the priest. They expected him to preach and say Mass!

The couple explained that they were not official ministers of the Church but were only a Franciscan couple come to visit their village. They explained that they could not say Mass, nor could they really be of much physical assistance on this short visit. But they could give them the most precious gift one human being can give to another: they could care, and care deeply! With these simple words the whole congregation began to shed tears of love and appreciation. Not one dry eye was left, including our Franciscan couple.

I believe this story tells of the greatest gift we can give to the poor. We can give them our hearts. It is like the story of St. Peter and St. John as they walked through the streets of Jerusalem. They met a cripple who begged for some money from them. Peter said to the cripple, "I have neither silver or gold, but what I have I give to you! In the name of Jesus Christ, the Nazarene, walk!" The cripple was immediately cured and began to walk and praise God.

It is more important to give the poor our hearts than to give them our money. If we give them our hearts we will change our lives for them. If we change our lives we will truly help them. But the greatest thing we can do is care. This shares the gospel of Jesus Christ with them more than millions of impersonal dollars. A heart that cares is a treasure beyond monetary value.

So in the face of this rampant fire of materialism we Western Christians must make some decisions. Will we propagate the madness, or will we change? We are either for materialism or against it. There is no middle ground. If we are for it, then we can continue as we have in the past. If we are against it, then we must change. We must change our life-styles. We must change our wants to be more in line with the needs of the needy. Most important of all, we must change our hearts.

St. Francis

Francis of Assisi stands as an example of a man who followed Jesus' call to "change," or repent, without compromise. He changed his heart and his life to be conformed totally to the sacred heart and life of our Lord Jesus Christ. Thomas of Celano writes, "The soul of Francis melted toward the poor. . . . Whatever he saw in anyone of want, he transferred in his mind, by a quick change, to Christ. Thus, in all the poor he saw the Son of the poor lady, and he bore naked in his heart him whom she bore naked in her hands."

Francis defended the rights of the poor to the extent that, if he had something that they did not, he considered it their rightful possession. But he did not defend their rights by force or even by political revolution. He defended their rights by sacrificing his own. Bonaventure writes, "Francis saw Christ's image in every poor person he met and he was prepared to give them everything he had, even if he himself had urgent need of it. He even believed they had a right to such alms, as if they belonged to them." Francis said, "God the great Almsgiver will regard it a theft on my part if I do not give what I have to someone who needs it more."

Do we steal the needs of the needy by refusing to give up our wants? According to Francis they belong by right to the poor. Do we defend their rights, or abuse them? According to Jesus Himself, they belong to Him, for He is the poor. Do we give to Jesus in need, or do we deprive Him? These are serious questions that demand answers serious enough to change our entire lives. Only by changing our own personal lives can we ever expect to change the world.

The only way to change the fire of materialism is by embracing the poverty of the gospel like a flame of love. This kind of poverty does not oppress. It sets us free! It is not a curse. It is a blessing of the richest kind. As Jesus Himself says, "Blessed are the poor."

Francis embraced this gospel poverty like a passionate lover: "Looking upon poverty as especially dear to the Son of God, though it was spurned throughout the whole world, he sought to

17

espouse her in perpetual charity. Therefore, after he had become a lover of her beauty, he put aside all things that he might cling to her more closely as his spouse and that 'they might be two in one' (Gen. 2:24) spirit. Therefore he gathered her to himself with chaste embraces and not even for an hour did he allow himself not to be her husband."

For Francis the espousal of Lady Poverty was the only way to defeat the lustful fire of materialism that destroys both body and soul. Bonaventure says, "His love for absolute poverty constituted a special privilege which enabled him to grow rich in spiritual wealth." Francis used to say, "Believe me, my brothers, poverty is the special way of salvation. It is the source of all humility and the root of all perfection and its fruit is manifold, though unseen. This is the treasure hidden in the field in the Gospel to buy which we must sell all—and anything that cannot be sold should be abandoned for love of it."

Do not be deceived. Materialism is a fire that destroys. It destroys the bodies of the poor, and it consumes the souls of the rich. James says, "It will devour your flesh like a fire." It is the root of all war. James says again, "Where do the conflicts and disputes among you originate? Is it not your inner cravings that make war within your members? What you desire you do not obtain, and so you resort to murder."

Government

If we want to do away with war, we must first do away with materialism. The messianic kingdom spoken of by the prophet Isaiah is a kingdom of peace because it is first a kingdom of justice. He says, "One nation shall not raise the sword against another, nor shall they train for war again." But he first says, "He shall judge between the nations, and impose terms on many peoples." He indirectly proclaims that all will be fed properly when he says,

"They shall beat their swords into plowshares and their spears into pruning hooks." He says elsewhere of the equality of labor and distribution of wealth: "They shall live in the houses they build, and eat the fruit on the vineyards they plant; they shall not build houses for others to live in, or plant for others to eat." If we are going to establish peace, we must stamp out materialism. Materialism breeds inequality, and inequality breeds war!

It is ironic that the "born-again" Christians now have "their man in office." Yet it is this very government that deprives the poor in order to build the machinery of war. It is indifferent to poverty on the one hand and prepares for war on the other. Ironically it is this government that consistently stands for such anti-Christian principles.

Isaiah speaks of a spirituality that prays much but does little. "When you spread out your hands, I close my eyes to you; Though you pray all the more, I will not listen. Your hands are full of blood! Wash yourselves clean!... Make justice your aim: redress the wronged, hear the orphan's plea, defend the widow. Come now, let us set things right, says the Lord: Though your sins be like scarlet, they may become white as snow."

Ironically, our "born-again" government does the opposite of the scriptural command. It has cut off a great deal of federal aid to the poor. Our streets are filled with the mentally disoriented and the elderly who find themselves suddenly homeless. Our cities pass laws making it impossible for these people to find homes or even to stay warm. In an attempt to clean up the inner cities the wealthy have been invited back in to refurbish the old tenement houses of the slums. This all sounds fine, but it totally displaces the poor who once lived there. Now the poor find themselves on the street with no place to go. To make matters worse, the cities pass ordinances making it illegal for the homeless and the poor to get warm even on the airvent grates or in the subway exits. Many die unprotected and homeless in the harsh cold of the winter snows.

Our present approach to government places the responsibility of these homeless and poor in the private sector. According to our government, it is up to the churches and nonprofit organizations to deal with this problem. Our government claims that it was not part of the original vision of our Founding Fathers to support the poor. In a very real sense our government is right!

According to the founding principles of this nation, taxation was only for the purpose of providing a strong defense. All other social or religious charity was left to the private sector. In an attempt to return to those ideals, our present administration is cutting back on social-aid programs. Besides, the cutbacks help to balance the federal budget. If we are going to spend on defense, we have to cut back on social programs. In fact, it was not until Franklin D. Roosevelt's "New Deal" that the federal government began really to become actively involved in these social concerns. It must be admitted that, along with its benefits, the programs involve high taxes and a frequently imbalanced budget.

This places today's committed Christian in an interesting dilemma. We recognize the need for some defense, but we also recognize the need for social programs. Like everyone else, we like low taxes. But the consistent historical approach of the Church toward governments is to encourage the common good of those they govern. Thus, the Church supports governments that are concerned for their own poor and for the poor of the world. Our present administration falls almost criminally short in this area and is still unable markedly to lower taxes or balance the federal budget!

For the biblical and Catholic Christian it is beyond political questions of the Left or the Right. It is not a matter of being Democratic or Republican. Neither party represents the full biblical perspective of the Christian mind. Some Republican politicians share our stance on pro-life and other domestic moral issues. But some do not at all represent our view toward God's just government in concern for the poor. This holds true within our own borders and in our foreign policy. We help to oppress the poor by supporting policies and foreign governments that oppress the poor. The Democrats might better represent the Catholic Christian mind in this area, but they sometimes stand squarely against its pro-life position. As a biblical and Catholic Christian, I am not comfortable with either the Republican or the Democrat *per se.* Neither always represents the mind of the Church. Neither always does the will of God.

Perhaps we need a third option in the nation. Maybe it is time to move beyond the vision of the Founding Fathers of this country to better accommodate the prophetic unfolding of the vision of the Spirit of God.

I believe that the quality of human governments evolves under the providence of God. The United States emerged as a higher form of government than has ever existed before on the face of the earth. It was more free. It was more godly. Its courts were fairer and its wars less self-centered. Our people have always been moral and charitable. I am, indeed, proud to be an American, a citizen of the United States. But I also realize that it might be time for the Christians of the world to take a step up higher. It might be time more fully to manifest the moral teachings of Jesus Christ within the just governments of the lands and nations within which we dwell.

I am not saying that we will bring perfect peace through a civil government. As long as sin exists in the world, we will not experience perfect and total peace anywhere. Nor am I saying that we will bring inner conversion through external means. I am aware, however, that one can raise the moral consciousness of a people by raising the moral quality of its government and laws. These external measures prepare the way for the internal conversion. They act as the Old Testament Law did for the Jews. They can be "schoolmasters" to prepare an entire nation, in fact the entire world, for the peaceful reign of Jesus Christ.

I write this as a poor Franciscan Brother. I have no desire to enter the world of politics. For me the gentle revolution of which I write remains a spiritual one. It is built from the inside out. It is ruled only by the indwelling of Jesus Christ within each individual human soul. The Church alone remains the primary expression of this kingdom on the face of the earth.

I do, however, see the exciting possibility of others more qualified than myself entering into the political world in order to take up this challenge. Perhaps we need a new Christian socialism. I am not talking about an atheistic or humanistic socialism. I am talking about a *Christian* socialism that builds on and protects basic, inalienable human rights for both the rich *and* the poor— God's just government that cares for the poor of this world while defending the freedom of all. It has never existed before on the face of the earth.

God challenges us to take up this call as biblical and Catholic Christians. He challenges us who live in the secular world to bring the gospel of Jesus Christ to this nation's poor and to the poor of all the world. He challenges us to defend the basic human rights of all living souls, those in the womb and those already born into the world.

If our governments are really to represent the morality of the Christian people who live within their domain, they must listen to these pleas and change. If they will not, those qualified Christians must take up the challenge of public office in order to preserve the inalienable rights of basic human life. The fire of God burns without compromise.

3
The Fire of Lust

St. James says that materialism is a destructive fire. We have seen that it causes poverty, and that both materialism and poverty are primary causes of war. It is interesting that James also sees a link between materialism and lust as a cause of war. He says, "Where do conflicts and disputes among you originate? Is it not your inner cravings that make war within your members? What you desire you do not obtain, and so you resort to murder." Some translations, such as the King James Version, speak of these inner cravings as actual lust. So as the fire of materialism is a very real cause for war in this world, so too is human lust.

The fire of lust has, no doubt, been experienced by every one of us. The scriptures often speak of lust as a fire. Regarding heterosexual lust, St. Paul says, "To those not married and to widows I have this to say: It would be well if they remain as they are, even as I do myself, but if they cannot exercise self-control, they should marry. It is better to marry than to be on fire."

The book of Proverbs speaks of the lust of adultery: "Lust not in your heart after her beauty, let her not captivate you with her glance! Can a man take fire to his bosom, and his garments not be burned? Or can a man walk on live coals, and his feet not be scorched? So with him who goes in to his neighbor's wife."

St. Paul also speaks clearly of the lust of homosexuality. "They claimed to be wise, but turned into fools instead.... God delivered them up in their lusts to unclean practices; they engaged in mutual degradation of their bodies.... Their women exchanged natural intercourse for unnatural, and the men gave up natural intercourse with women and burned with lust for one another."

The fire of sexual immorality is, indeed, a hot topic in the Church today! Some theologians and pastors are so liberal that they simply say that almost anything is permissible if it is done in "love." Others are so conservative and have so tightly grasped the cold legal prohibitions against sexual immorality that they have forgotten that the greatest of all Jesus' commandments *was* love.

I have a great many friends who have fallen to either side of the teachings of Jesus and the Church by embracing either extreme of liberal or conservative ideology. I have certainly caught myself tending toward one or the other of these judgmental extremes by finding the bad spiritual fruit they produce in my life. The fruit is like a gauge that reveals the quality of the ideology I am rooted in. When I am overly conservative, I find that even the correct law of God slowly takes the place of God so that I commit a subtle idolatry. Even though I do this in the name of God, it still remains sinful thinking. I have conserved a law but lost my soul! Likewise when I am overly liberal, I rationalize the clear law of God to accommodate my own human sin, thus committing idolatry once more by making a god of my sin. Here my primary motivation for liberalizing my theology is the refusal to let go of both my sin and of God, thus necessitating that I remake God according to the image of my sin. This, too, is idolatry. I must either let go of sin or let go of God. I cannot possess them both. It is far better that, in all cases, He remake me according to His image after the pattern of the image of His Son.

From my personal experience, I have observed that when I allow the fire of lust to burn within my heart, I lose the spiritual "edge" in my soul. One desert father says that the demons of lust and fornication dull our sharp eagerness to pray. When I allow myself to fantasize sexually, I find that the fantasies will grow stronger until they grip and strangle the breath of the Spirit from my soul. You cannot keep illicit fantasies in check. They must either grow weak or grow stronger. They cannot stand still in the human soul.

St. Paul speaks of this consuming nature of the fire of lust and sexual immorality when he says, "Put to death whatever in your nature is rooted in earth: fornication, uncleanliness, passion, evil desires, and that lust which is idolatry. These are the sins which provoke God's wrath. Your own conduct was once of this sort,

when these sins were your very life." By their nature they become our "very life"!

It is true that the fire of lust has a way of taking over a person's life. We begin with fantasies and end in actions. The actions re-enforce the fantasies and a vicious cycle begins. Soon, both our thoughts and our actions are controlled by a sexual lust. Rather than using our sexuality properly to bring forth health and life in Christ and to glorify God, we allow lust to lead to sickness and death.

St. James speaks of the downward spiral of lust when he says, "God, who is beyond the grasp of evil, tempts no one. Rather, the tug and lure of his own passion tempt every man. Once passion has conceived, it gives birth to sin, and when sin reaches maturity it begets death." If fantasies and sexual immorality live in us, then our spiritual life must die. If our spiritual life is to live, our fantasies and life of sexual immorality must die. One has only to think of the tragic victims of sex-related diseases to see this scripture graphically realized. The ominous warning of this scripture is no joke. God is quite serious.

Furthermore, most of our fiery sexual fantasies are pure illusion. Many of them involve people and situations that will never be actually lived out. They disturb our spiritual peace and excite us to no fulfilling end. They are really a waste of precious energy and time.

As St. Paul says, "You must no longer live as the pagans do. They have abandoned themselves to lust and the indulgence of every sort of lewd conduct.... You must lay aside your former way of life and the old self which deteriorates through illusion and desire."

Most of our fantasies will never come true and the fantasies that are lived out do not bring healthy, life-giving, love relationships. By and large they bring only emotional pain. Some even bring physical sickness and death. All of this is the work of a devil whose only intent is to bring pain and death into a world created by God. Jesus says of the devil, "He brought death to man from the beginning, and has never based himself on the truth; the truth is not in him. Lying speech is his native tongue; he is a liar and the father of lies." Yet Jesus says of Himself, "I have come that they might have life and have it to the full." The way of Jesus brings life. It is true and eternally real. The way of the devil is an illusion at best. It is a lie that brings forth eventual death.

The sad part is that the devil disguises himself as an instrument of God. He says he is good and true. He says he brings life. He says that lust and sexual immorality are really a free expression of God's love. Do not be deceived. It is a lie!

Unfortunately this even happens within the Church. Many theologians and ministers propagate an unduly permissive morality in the name of God's love. It is true that James says, "Wisdom from above us...peaceable, lenient, docile, rich in sympathy," but Paul also says of love, "Love does not rejoice in what is wrong, but rejoices with the truth." The teaching of the Church remains true, but her ministers sometimes mislead us into error.

St. Paul had the same problem in his day: "My fear is that, just as the serpent seduced Eve by his cunning, your thoughts may be corrupted and you may fall away from your sincere and complete devotion to Christ. I say this because, when someone comes preaching another Jesus than the one we preached, or when you receive a different spirit than the one you have received, or a gospel other than the gospel you accepted, you seem to endure it quite well.... Such men are false apostles of Christ. And little wonder! For even Satan disguises himself as an angel of light."

Again, Paul says to the Ephesians, "As for lewd conduct or promiscuousness or lust of any sort, let them not even be mentioned among you; your holiness forbids this.... Make no mistake about this: no fornicator, no unclean or lustful person—in effect an idolator—has any inheritance in the kingdom of Christ and of God. Let no one deceive you with worthless arguments."

Today there are many arguments in the Church about sexuality. Certainly not all are invalid, but they can be confusing. For the average lay person it can be very difficult to distinguish between valid questions and worthless arguments. Most people simply love God and want to do the right thing. They have neither the time nor the inclination to do even a basic Bible study, much less a theological investigation about sexual temptations. They rely on the Church to give them clear yet loving answers.

The Teaching of the Church

The Catholic Church has spoken very clearly on these issues in the *Declaration on Certain Questions Concerning Sexual Ethics*, by the Sacred Congregation for the Doctrine of the Faith on December 29, 1975. Aware of the confusion concerning sexuality, it says, "The Church cannot remain indifferent to this confusion of minds and relaxation of morals. It is a question, in fact, of a matter which is of utmost importance both for the personal lives of Christians and for the social life of our time." On the question of the authority of the Church to put forward an absolute teaching about sexual morals, the document says: "Hence, those many people are in error who today assert that one can find neither in human nature nor in the revealed law any absolute or immutable norm to serve for particular actions other than the one which expresses itself in the general law of charity and respect for human dignity."

Many people accept Jesus' or Paul's teachings on sexuality as being only relative applications of the general law of love in particular cultural settings at that time. They deny that scripture can speak to the particular sexual problems of our modern world. Thus, in some settings pre- or extramarital sex may be wrong, but in others it may be acceptable. The same would hold true for homosexuality or masturbation. The Church responds: "As proof of their assertation they put forward the view that so called norms of the natural law or precepts of Sacred Scripture are to be regarded only as given expressions of a form of particular culture at a certain moment of history. . . . Now the Church throughout her history has always considered a certain number of precepts of the natural law as having an absolute and immutable value, and in their transgression she has seen a contradiction of the teaching and spirit of the Gospel. (Since sexual ethics concern certain fundamental values of human and Christian life, this general teaching applies equally to sexual ethics.) In this domain there exist principles and norms which the Church has already unhesitantly transmitted as part of her teachings, however much the opinions and morals of the world may have been opposed to them. . . . They therefore cannot be considered as having become out of date or doubtful under the pretext that a new cultural situation has arisen."

The Church unhesitatingly reaffirms that all genital sex acts must take place within the context of marriage. "Today there are many who vindicate the right to sexual union before marriage. . . . This opinion is contrary to Christian doctrine, which states that every genital act must be within the framework of marriage."

The moral goodness of genital sex involves "the finality of the sexual act." This "finality" is composed of "mutual self-giving and human procreation in the context of true love." Sex that is morally good must include the natural possibility for procreation as well as the opportunity intimately to express love for another human being. Without both of these, the sexual act of marriage loses its sacramental character in which the love between Jesus and the Church is fully symbolized and consumated in sexual union. Because of this, homosexuality is not a complete expression of good Christian sex. Likewise, masturbation is seen as an incomplete expression of it.

As to homosexual relations: "At the present time there are those who, basing themselves on observations in the psychological order, have begun to judge indulgently, and even to excuse completely, homosexual relations between certain people. This they do in opposition to the constant teaching of the Magisterium and to the moral sense of the Christian people." The Church does recognize the reality of homosexuality and counsels a respect of basic human rights toward homosexuals and the constant presence of Christian love. "Some persons find themselves through no fault of their own to have a homosexual orientation. Homosexuals, like everyone else, should not suffer from prejudice against their basic human rights. They have a right to respect, friendship and justice. They should have an active role in the Christian community. Homosexual activity, however, as distinguished from homosexual orientation, is morally wrong. . . . Because heterosexuals can usually look forward to marriage, and homosexuals, while their orientation continues, might not, the Christian community should provide them a special degree of pastoral understanding and care." (*To Live in Christ Jesus*, National Conference of Catholic Bishops, November 11, 1976.)

Masturbation is also treated clearly: "The traditional Catholic doctrine that masturbation constitutes a grave moral disorder is often called into doubt or expressly denied today. . . . Even if it cannot be proved that Scripture condemns this sin by name, the tradition of the Church has rightly understood it to be condemned in the New Testament when the letter speaks of 'impurity,' 'unchasteness,' and other vices contrary to chastity and continence."

Many people point to the frequency of the above practices as proof of their rightness in the natural moral order. Speaking specifically of this within the context of masturbation, the Church says, "Sociological surveys are able to show the frequency of this disorder according to the places, populations or circumstances studied. In this way facts are discovered, but facts do not constitute a criterion for judging the moral value of human acts. The frequency of the phenomenon in question is certainly to be linked with man's innate weakness following original sin; but it is also linked with the loss of a sense of God, with the corruption of morals engendered by the commercialization of vice, with the unrestrained licentiousness of so many public entertainments and publications, as well as with the neglect of modesty, which is the guardian of chastity." As stated above, even when the opinion of the world has differed with the teaching of the Church, she must hold on to gospel truths. The truth of the gospel will never change, and the truth will set us free.

With all of these teachings of the Church toward sexual ethics, the attitude of love must be maintained. We may rightly call a sexual act a sin, but we must genuinely love the sinner through it all. Many so-called Christians, however, say "I hate the sin, but love the sinner," but in fact hate only *some* sins. A heterosexual Christian might easily forgive the heterosexual sinner, but, in his heart, harbor hatred for the homosexual sinner. Such inequalities are sins themselves! James says, "Whoever falls into sin on one point of the law, even though he keeps the entire remainder, has become guilty on all counts." Those who sin heterosexually are no better than the homosexual sinner. He or she who masturbates is no less guilty than those who sexually sin with a partner. And those who judge are also sinners. Sin is equal for us all.

This should lead us to an attitude of unconditional love. We should approach sexual sins with the clarity of truth, but also with the understanding of compassion and love. Jesus did say, "You will know the truth and the truth will set you free," but he also said to the woman caught in the act of adultery, "Nor do I condemn you. You may go." And then He added, "But from now on, avoid this sin." The teaching of the Church is like this. It does not, and should not, compromise on objective moral truths. These truths set people free from the misguided direction of sin. But these truths must always be shared in understanding and unconditional love.

A problem arises when the ministers of the Church give personal opinions rather than the Church's teaching. The average person first wants to know: Is masturbation O.K.? Is extra- and premarital sex O.K.? Is homosexuality O.K.? They just want an answer, "yes" or "no," then counsel, encouragement, and forgiveness when they fail. St. Paul says, "As God keeps his word, I declare that my word to you is not 'yes' one minute and 'no' the next." The Church gives clear teaching based on both scripture and tradition about most of these things. Her ministers would serve the people of God much better by lovingly, but consistently, passing on her teaching both in letter and in spirit.

The Fire of Lust

The basic gospel message about reforming your life is a positive message! To turn from the so-called blessings of "free love," or sexual immorality of any kind, is not bad news. It is good news! Free love is not freedom. Promiscuity and masturbation do not really fulfill. All of these are misdirected expressions of sexuality that enslave us to a lust that can destroy our whole life.

The Law and the Spirit

Yet it is never enough simply to be told that these things are wrong. *We must replace them with something that is right.* We must replace the fire of lust with the fire of God. Otherwise we fall into a legalism that only represses our sexuality rather than redirecting and fulfilling it according to God's plan. It is true that the lust of sexual immorality brings death, but so does a gospel that is no better than legalism. As St. Paul says, "It was only through the law that I came to know sin.... The commandment that should have led to life brought me death.... I do not do what I want to do but what I hate.... So with my mind I serve the law of God but with my flesh the law of sin."

It is not enough simply to know what is "wrong." We must be empowered with "right." Even though I know lust is wrong, I cannot get free of its grip. The more I know it is wrong and am unable to do what is right, the more guilt-ridden and depressed I become. The more depressed I get the more unable I am to get free.

The law of the Church, left to itself, cannot free me from the fire of lust and sin. It may be clearly taught by its ministers. It may make perfect sense to me. But left to itself, even the correct law of God will lead me to eventual death. If both the lust of sin and the law of God can lead me to death, how can I be set free? As Paul says, "What a wretched man I am! Who can free me from this body under the power of death?" The answer is to experience and express the fire of the Holy Spirit, which frees us from the gripping

31

fire of lust. When the Holy Spirit comes into our lives in its full power, all grave sin simply falls away.

We are like one vessel which cannot contain full measures of any two liquids at once. In Christ the water of the Holy Spirit is poured into the cup of our life, which is often filled with the flaming oil of lust. When God pours the Spirit fully into our life by its nature, the oil of sin is displaced and the destructive fire of lust is put out. If the Spirit is dwelling powerfully within us, the lust of sin will be displaced by an ardent passion for God.

St. Paul speaks of this when he says, "The law of the spirit, the spirit of life in Christ Jesus, has freed you from the law of sin and death. The law was powerless because of its weakening by the flesh. . . . Those who live according to the flesh are intent on the things of the flesh, those who live according to the spirit, on those of the spirit. . . . The flesh in its tendency is at enmity with God; it is not subject to God's law. Indeed, it cannot be; those who are in the flesh cannot please God. But you are not in the flesh; you are in the spirit, since the Spirit of God dwells in you." He concludes this thought in his letter to the Galatians: "My point is that you should live in accord with the spirit and you will not yield to the cravings of the flesh." As St. Bonaventure says, "It seems amazing that we should be so deeply concerned about frivolous and perishable things of this world. . . . I can see no other explanation than that our love for God has turned to frost and ice within us. Most certainly, if we were burning with love, we would shed our worldly garments to follow the naked Christ." Or again, "As wax melts before the fire, so vice perishes before love. Such is the power of love that it alone closes hell, opens heaven, restores the hope of salvation, and makes a soul agreeable to God." Yet again, "When we are inflamed with the ardor of such celestial desire . . . the whole world seems bitter and tiresome." If the fire of the Spirit is stirred within our lives, the lusts of the flesh and the desires for sexual immorality simply fall away and lose their grip on our lives or their burning fire that parches the soul.

How do we receive the Holy Spirit? The scriptures say it is as

simple as asking! Jesus says, "Ask and you shall receive; seek and you shall find; knock and it shall be opened to you.... If you, with all your sins, know how to give your children good things, how much more will the heavenly Father give the Holy Spirit to those who ask Him."

It is true that many of us have sacramentally received the Holy Spirit through Baptism and Confirmation, but that does not keep us from the need of daily asking to experience actively the presence of the Spirit in our life. Jesus said that we must make a decision to follow Him daily, not just once a long time ago. Paul encourages those who have already received the Spirit to continue in and grow into its fullness. He writes to Timothy, "For this reason I remind you to stir into flame the gift of God bestowed when my hands were laid on you. The Spirit God has given us is no cowardly spirit, but rather one that makes us strong, loving and wise."

Have you really asked for the Holy Spirit with your whole heart? Have you experienced this initial freedom from the fire of lust, or does it still grip you and choke the life from your soul? Can anyone write progressive books on moral theology if he has never experienced the age-old power of the Spirit of God in his life? Without the Spirit, all of our theological explanations are either too strict or too vague. We cannot be progressive unless we conserve this power too great for even all the world to contain. Ask for the Spirit and you will be free. Do not be afraid to get excited about God. Be on fire! The words of Paul to Timothy indicate that you must make an effort fully to receive this gift. The words of Jesus say that you must ask. St. James says, "Draw close to God, and He will draw close to you." Make an effort to receive this gift. God made an effort to give it to you. He drew close to you in Jesus Christ. Jesus asks that the Father give Him disciples. Draw close to God and ask Him for the fire of Spirit with all your heart.

Renewal of the Mind

But how do we draw close to God? How do we ask? Do we just ask God for the Spirit and wait for the spiritual fireworks to go off, or are there specific things to do to accommodate the coming of the fire of the Spirit? Scripture and tradition would both say there are specific ways to cooperate with the movement of the Spirit. As Paul says, "Stir into flame the gift of God bestowed when my hands were laid upon you." There are ways to stir up the fire of the Spirit. It is already given to most of us in Baptism and Confirmation. Now we must simply stir up the gift!

The battleground of the fire of lust begins in the human mind. There are many battles and wars that face the human race today. The nuclear arms race, human rights, and world poverty are all battles that face our apparently comfortable Western world. Yet the battle for the human mind is even more basic and more primary. It is in our minds that faith and morals are conceptualized. It is from the mind that our actions of the future are formulated in the present. Without first winning the battle for the mind we will never be able to meet the external moral battles that face our world. Without first dealing with the battles of lust in our minds we will never be able to bring social justice or peace. As St. James says, "Where do the conflicts and disputes among you originate? Is it not your inner cravings that make war within your members?"

Paul speaks of the Holy Spirit having a definite effect on our minds. "You must lay aside your former way of life and the old self which deteriorates through illusion and desire, and acquire a fresh, spiritual way of thinking. You must put on that new man created in God's image whose justice and holiness are born of truth."

For Paul the battle against the illusions created by lust begin in the mind. The truly spiritual mind is directed toward the truth. It is in the mind that the popular concepts of the world must be laid aside. It is in the mind that new ones must be picked up. Likewise, the work of justice is here linked to a holiness rooted in the truth that is contemplated in the mind.

The Fire of Lust

He says to the Romans, "And now, brothers, I beg you through the mercy of God to offer your bodies as a living sacrifice holy and acceptable to God, your spiritual worship. Do not conform yourselves to this age but be transformed by the renewal of your mind, so that you may judge what is God's will, what is good, pleasing and perfect."

Here, the same Paul who speaks against sexual immorality says the transformation of our actions begins with the transformation of our thoughts. He also says this means being a nonconformist with the thoughts and actions of the world. The only way not to conform to the world in your actions is by conforming to God in your thoughts.

The thoughts of lust and sexual immorality work in the opposite way. Paul says to the Ephesians, "You must no longer live as the pagans do—their minds empty, their understanding darkened. They are estranged from God because of their ignorance and their resistance; without remorse they have abandoned themselves to lust and the indulgence of every sort of lewd conduct."

Paul speaks similarly about homosexual lust: "Their thinking became futile and their foolish hearts were darkened. Although they claimed to be wise, they became fools. . . . Therefore God gave them over in the sinful desires of their hearts to sexual impurity for the degrading of their bodies with one another. . . . God gave them over to shameful lusts. Even their women exchanged natural relations for unnatural ones. In the same way the men also abandoned natural relations with women and were inflamed with lust for one another. . . . Since they did not think it worthwhile to retain the knowledge of God, he gave them over to a depraved mind, to do what ought not to be done."

There is a definite connection between thoughts, emotions, and actions. Thoughts of sexual immorality lead to lust, and lust leads to sinful action. If we control our thoughts we will control our lust, and if we can control our lust we will control our actions.

Jesus says, "From the mind stem evil designs." He also says, "Wherever your treasure lies, there your heart will be." For many of us, our private thoughts or fantasies are our treasure. We do not

35

want to sin, but we do not want to give up our private fantasies either! We want to sell all we have and give to the poor radically to follow Jesus, but we will not give up our private sexual fantasies that are by their nature sinful and corrupt.

There is a great value to dreams and fantasies when they are pure and beautiful, but when they are clearly sinful and immoral they can be very harmful. This does not mean that sexual temptations will never come into our minds. Wild sexual thoughts will often pop into our minds seemingly out of nowhere. More than likely they will be both heterosexual and homosexual in nature. This is really quite normal and should not upset us. Tempting thoughts are not sinful. It is what we do with them that often makes them sinful. James says, "Once passion has conceived, it gives birth to sin." If we allow our tempting thoughts to conceive, then our actual thoughts are sinful. Do we feed the thoughts? Do we linger on them? Then they lead to lust. But do not be deceived here: The death grip of uncontrolled lust will follow your uncontrolled thoughts.

This is why Paul says, "Finally, my brothers, your thoughts should be wholly directed to all that is true, all that deserves respect, all that is honest, pure, admirable, decent, virtuous, or worthy of praise. Live according to what you have learned and accepted, what you have heard me say and seen me do." Paul tells us that we are actually to have the "mind of Christ." Notice the connection between thinking and living!

The role of the scriptures is very important here. The psalmist says, "Happy the man who . . . delights in the law of the Lord and meditates on his law day and night." Paul says to Timothy, "All scripture is inspired of God and is useful for . . . training in holiness." If we fill our minds with the pure things of God found in scripture, our life will be pure. If we fill our minds with the life of Christ as found in the gospels, our life will become like Christ. If we meditate on the life of Christ we will have the mind of Christ. This will change the fire of lust to the fire of love that will explode through our life with the power of the Holy Spirit.

We should take time every day prayerfully to read the scripture. An old saying goes, "Seven days without Bible reading makes one weak." A new one likens our mind to a computer program: "Garbage in, garbage out." The daily reading of scripture replaces the garbage with the spiritual bread of finest wheat. When this bread is digested it travels throughout our whole body to make us healthy and strong.

A young priest told me of some advice an elder priest once shared with him. If you want to remain faithful to your call, celebrate Mass with the Church every day, and read from the gospels and the letters of Paul in your private time every day. He told the young man to read the scripture, not intellectually like a cold-hearted scholar but like a personal love letter from God. Read in faith. That way most of the messages become simple and clear. It is only the pseudo-scholar who reads like a devil's advocate, doubting the obvious meaning of the words. Scholarship is good in its proper place, but pursued without Faith, it can lead the scholar to lose that Faith. Do not let that happen to you.

Power of Praise

How does the Holy Spirit control our thoughts? We know that it is impossible to control our actions just because we know them to be wrong: it is also equally impossible to control the fantasies of the mind. We may be able to control our thoughts while we read scripture, but as soon as we put the Bible down, the "old thoughts" assail us again. Even during Bible-reading, sexual thoughts can assail us. We may know very well from scripture that it is wrong to dwell on and enjoy the sexual temptations that pop into our minds: but most of us find ourselves powerless not to pursue a sexual fantasy. Left to itself the mind is powerless to control impure thoughts.

I have found that it is only with the power of praise and thanksgiving that I can control my mind. The only way to clear my mind of uncontrollable sexual fantasies is literally to flood my mind with God. For me this happens primarily through spontaneous, vibrant praise and thanksgiving offered to God.

Scripture tells us that the mind is renewed by the Holy Spirit, but it also tells us we must stir up the flame of the Spirit. This "stirring up" is frequently done through intentional praise. The psalmist says that we "enter his gates with thanksgiving, his courts with praise." Again and again the scriptures encourage, even command us, to "praise God." It stirs up the Holy Spirit!

In Paul's letters to the Ephesians and the Colossians he lists the vices that inflict us all: "fornication, uncleanliness, passion, evil desires and that lust which is idolatry." He then lists the virtues. But the key to living these listed virtues is not just in *knowing* what is right and wrong. This "law" cannnot save us any more than the "law" of the Old Testament. The key is *thanksgiving* and *praise!*

At the end of this whole section in Ephesians Paul says, "Be filled with the Holy Spirit, addressing one another in psalms and hymns and inspired songs. Sing praise to the Lord with all your hearts. Give thanks to God the Father always and for everything in the name of our Lord Jesus Christ." To the Colossians he says, "Dedicate yourselves to thankfulness. . . . Sing gratefully to God from your hearts in psalms, hymns, and inspired songs." Here the "word of Christ" comes to dwell deeply in us only through singing the word of God in praise. The word without the Spirit is useless. It is praise that stirs the Spirit, and the Spirit fills our mind, heart, and soul with God's word.

We read in the Roman Breviary a quote from St. Augustine: "Our thoughts in this present life should turn on the praise of God, because it is in praising God that we shall rejoice forever in the life to come. . . . Now therefore, brethren, we urge you to praise God. That is what we are telling each other when we say 'Alleluia.' You say to your neighbor, 'Praise the Lord!' and he says the same to you. . . . But see that your praise comes from your whole being: in other words, see that you praise God not with your lips and voices alone, but with your minds, your lives, and all your actions. . .

as our ears hear each other's voices, so do God's ears hear our thoughts." Here we see clearly that praise definitely affects our thoughts. Praise will come forth from our lips, but it must first inhabit our thoughts. It must affect our "whole being." If this praise is in our thoughts, then it will affect our whole life. If praise is truly in our life, then it will rise up to the very ears of God.

In the same book of prayer, Diadochus of Photice says, "Only the Holy Spirit can purify the mind. . . . We must try to provide the Holy Spirit with a resting place. Then we shall have the light of knowledge shining within us at all times, and it will show up for what they are all the dark and hateful temptations that come from demons, and not only will it show them up: exposure to this glorious light will also greatly diminish their power."

The Holy Spirit purifies the mind, and praise of God must come first from our thoughts. This means that the work of the Spirit is closely connected to praise of God. Praise bursts forth spontaneously when individuals are touched by the Spirit.

In the scriptural infancy narratives, praise bursts forth from those who are touched by the Holy Spirit. Elizabeth says to Mary, "Blest are you among women and blest is the fruit of your womb." When she is filled with the Holy Spirit, Mary responds with that beautiful hymn of praise, the "Magnificat," for the Holy Spirit, too, has overshadowed her. Zechariah, even though struck mute for lack of faith, has his tongue loosed to praise and bless "the God of Israel" in a prophecy because he is filled with the Holy Spirit. Simeon praised the God of the Jews and the Gentiles when he saw the infant Jesus, for the "Holy Spirit was upon him." All scripture is filled with similar connections between the Holy Spirit and outbursts of praise.

Paul not only tells us "do not stifle the Spirit" when it wells up from within, he also tells us to "stir into flame" the gift of the Holy Spirit. If the Spirit is so closely connected to praise and thanksgiving, one sure way to stir up the Spirit is by stirring up praise.

This means we must praise God even when we don't necessarily feel like it. We might feel awful. We might be burning up with the fire of lust and sin. God might be the farthest thing from our thoughts. We might even consider ourselves eternally lost. This is precisely the time to praise God! It is praise that stirs up the fire of the Spirit, which can purge our thoughts and hearts from the burning grip of lust and sin.

St. Augustine continues, "Let us sing alleluia here on earth, while we still live in anxiety, so that we may sing it one day in heaven in full security.... Even here amidst trials and temptations let us sing alleluia.... So, then, my brothers, let us sing now, not in order to enjoy a life of leisure, but in order to lighten our labors." It is by singing praises to God in the midst of temptations that we will be freed of their heaviness within our souls.

The prophet Habakkuk says, "For though the fig trees have no fruit and no grapes grow on the vines, even though the olive crop fails and the fields produce no grain, even though the sheep all die and the cattle stalls are empty, I will be joyful and glad, because God is my savior." Even though the "fruit of the Spirit" seems to be totally absent from our lives, we must still praise and thank God!

We might be enslaved to lust and sin. Our lives might be on fire and consumed with sexual immorality. We might spend our time telling others God says these things are "O.K.," knowing deep down inside they are wrong. This is precisely the time to thank and praise God! It is praise that stirs up the Spirit, and it is the Spirit that brings forth the good fruit of "love, joy, peace ... and chastity" in our lives. St. Paul says to the Romans, "We know that God makes all things work together for the good of those who have been called according to his decree." We can even praise God for the evil that comes into our lives! That's right. Even evil can work for our eventual good. Paul says, "Give thanks to God the Father always and for everything in the name of our Lord Jesus Christ." True, St. James says, "No one who is tempted is free to say, 'I am being tempted by God.' Surely God, who is beyond the grasp of evil, tempts no one." But even the evil the devil brings into our lives is turned against his purpose as soon as we turn to Christ. Satan cannot win if we are called by God. God allows us to learn from our mistakes and sins so that we might help others who are in sin. Paul says, "He comforts us in all our afflictions and thus enables us to comfort those who are in trouble, with the same consolation we have received from him." Praise God in, and even for, your sin and trouble; then you will be able to get free of it through the Spirit!

Tongues of Fire

I have often found the praise of God best expressed when I pray with the gift of tongues. The Acts of the Apostles clearly show that the phenomenon of tongues was an integral part of the giving of the Spirit to the Church on Pentecost. "Tongues as of fire appeared, which parted and came to rest on each of them. All were filled with the Holy Spirit. They began to express themselves in foreign tongues and make bold proclamations as the Spirit prompted them."

St. Paul devotes much of his first letter to the Corinthians to the charismatic gifts of the Spirit. The gift of tongues is undeniably included. "There are different gifts but the same Spirit. . . . To each person the manifestation of the Spirit is given for the common good. . . . One receives the gift of tongues, another that of interpreting the tongues. . . . Set your hearts on spiritual gifts. I should like it if all of you spoke in tongues. . . . Thank God, I speak in tongues more than any of you." Here, Paul speaks of the manifestation of tongues in the assembly, emphasizes the need for interpretation, and the preference for the gift of prophecy. It is clear, however, that tongues were an accepted part of the Corinthians' worship.

Paul also connects praise of God with both praying and singing in tongues. In treating the whole topic of tongues he suddenly says, "If I pray in a tongue my spirit is at prayer but my mind contributes nothing. What is my point here? I want to pray with the spirit, and also to pray with my mind. I want to sing with my spirit

41

and with my mind as well. If your praise of God is solely with the spirit, how will the one who does not comprehend be able to say 'Amen' to your thanksgiving?" Here, both prayer and singing in the Spirit are linked to praise, thanksgiving, and the understanding of the mind. But does praying and singing in the Spirit totally exclude the mind?

Eddie Ensley in his book *Sounds of Wonder* writes: "St. John Chrysostom says, 'It is permitted to sing psalms without words, so long as the mind resounds within.' True, as St. Paul says, praying or singing in tongues can bypass the mind, but tongues can also purify the mind. In a public gathering some interpretation is needed for tongues, but especially in private, praising God with tongues can be a powerful tool."

Sometimes our minds are so entrapped by sinful thoughts that we simply cannot break free. Tongues help break us free in the Spirit, and then the Spirit purifies the mind. But the Spirit cannot be released in our thoughts until we have prayed a prayer of praise that surpasses the thoughts. As Paul says to the Romans, "The Spirit too helps us in weakness, for we do not know how to pray as we ought; but the Spirit makes intercession for us with groanings that cannot be expressed in speech."

In *Sounds of Wonder*, we are reminded that "St. Augustine speaks of singing in tongues along a similar vein: 'Where speech does not suffice . . . they break into singing on vowel sounds.' He calls this 'jubilation,' and urges his listeners to stir up this gift. 'You already know what it is to jubilate. Rejoice and speak. If you cannot express your joy, jubilate. . . . He who sings a jubilus does not utter words; he pronounces a wordless sound of joy . . . he simply lets his joy burst forth without words; his voice then appears to express a happiness so intense that he cannot formulate it. . . . What is jubilation? Joy that cannot be expressed in words; yet the voice expresses what is conceived within and cannot be explained verbally; this is jubilation!' "

Many times persons trapped in lust and a life of various grave sins try to pray but simply cannot. The words won't come because

42

the thoughts are not free and clear. Their prayer can only be expressed with feelings. Somewhere down deep inside their spirit cries out to God, but in their minds they are still confused. This is when praying or singing in tongues can be a powerful tool in helping to free a person from total enslavement to sin. I have had many occasions to minister to people who are tired, burned out, emotionally and physically sick. Many seem near death. They try to pray but cannot. They try to break free but cannot. They try to praise God but cannot. In these cases it has only been praying in the wordless prayer and praise of tongues that has allowed them finally to reach out to God.

Burning Tears

Sometimes the only prayer a person can come up with is to cry. They cry and sob, and tears well up from deep inside. These tears are precious in God's eyes. They are in fact His gift. They help us pray and cleanse us from every sin. They put out the fire of lust that has often gripped us for so long.

When Jesus went to dine at a Pharisee's home, a woman known throughout the town as a sinner approached Him. Most have assumed she was probably a prostitute. As Jesus reclined at table, "She brought in a vase of perfumed oil and stood behind him at his feet, weeping so that her tears fell upon his feet. Then she wiped them with her hair, kissing them and perfuming them with oil." As far as we know this woman did not utter a word. All she did was cry, wipe Jesus' feet with her hair and kiss His feet with her lips. The Pharisee interpreted these acts as unclean and sensual. Jesus looked through her tears to her heart and said, "Her many sins are forgiven—because of her great love. . . . Your faith has been your salvation. Now go in peace."

Here the gift of tears is very similar to the gift of tongues. Both express a deep internal love and longing for Jesus that cannot be adequately expressed with words. Both speak more than a thousand eloquent words and can be clearly understood by God. Both can be a turning point for those who are living a life of sin.

Evagrius Ponticus, born A.D. 345, writes from the early monastic tradition in his books, *Praktikos* and *Chapters on Prayer*. Regarding the gift of tears he says, "Pray first for the gift of tears so that by means of sorrow you may soften your native rudeness. . . . Pray with tears and your request will find a hearing. Nothing so gratifies the Lord as supplication offered in the midst of tears."

St. Maximus, born A.D. 580, wrote of the gift of tears in the endeavor to overcome lust. "When the demons have thrown chastity out of your mind and surround you with thoughts of fornication, then with tears say to the Master, 'They have cast me forth and now they have surrounded me. My joy, deliver me from them that surround me.' And you will be safe."

St. Symeon, born A.D. 949, clearly connects tears to the fire of the Holy Spirit. "He who is interiorly illuminated by the Holy Spirit cannot bear the sight [the sudden streak of lightning flashes and the resplendence of the Spirit within]. . . . He becomes like one whose entrails are touched by fire, devoured by the flame, unable to endure the burning; he is beside himself and cannot contain himself, but sheds abundant tears which refresh him, and stir up the flame of his desire; then his tears become more abundant and, purified by this flood, he shines with much brilliancy. Then, wholly inflamed, he becomes like the light."

But Symeon distinguishes between the "way" of tears and the "gift" of tears. The *gift* of tears comes on you suddenly and overwhelms you. It is a gift of the Spirit and acts independently of our will. If it is given, then we must choose what to do with it. The *way* of tears is a matter of choice, of the will. Symeon says that we can choose the way of tears every day. Then the *way* of tears will often open us even more to the *gift* of tears. The way of tears should be sought, especially at the beginning of our conversion, so that we may stir up the gift of the Spirit. Then the Spirit will free our thoughts and actions from sin.

Symeon says, "Tears and compunction cleanse the house of the soul.... For without water it is impossible to wash a dirty garment, and without tears it is even more impossible to cleanse and purify the soul from its stains and dirt.... Let us seek this grace with our whole soul." He then brings back the image of fire: "For he who seeks it with his whole soul will find it; or, rather, it is virtue itself that will come and find him who seeks it, and had he a heart harder than bronze, barely has it found him before his heart becomes more pliant than wax. For it is the divine fire, which dispels mountains and rocks . . . and changes them into a kind of paradise, and transforms the souls who receive it. For within them it becomes a flowing stream, like living water."

Symeon says this flowing fire of tears should be sought every day, especially during the sacrament of Holy Communion. "Brother, never communicate without tears.... Let no one say it is impossible to weep every day.... For if you say it is impossible to shed tears every day, you say it is impossible to be humble and rejoice without ceasing in prayer, to obtain a heart free from all passions and evil thoughts in order to contemplate God."

Here we see again a prayer that surpasses thoughts working to free the mind of evil thoughts. In this, the way of tears is very similar to stirring up the gift of tongues. Both are a choice. Both include the mind but far surpass the mind. Both eventually free the mind of evil and replace it with a literal flood of the fiery light of God. When the mind is flooded with God's light, then we will see many issues of faith and morality differently. Then that which was once a burden for us to obey will become easy and light!

Before anyone understands through actual experience this holy fire, he or she cannot really be free of the fire of lust. They might believe in God. They might want to love Him. But without this fire of the Spirit, God's laws will always be seen as too burdensome actually to live. This will lead many to seek ways to rationalize God's truth to conform with their habitual experience of both mental and bodily impurity. They then make all moral truth relative to allow for their sin. The relativity of these situational ethics will eventually lead to even more despair. It will destroy individuals and nations and leave them wandering, aimless and blind, easy prey for the enemy of their souls.

It is only by the fire of the Spirit that we can know the truth that will set us free. Once we really experience and stir up the fire of the Spirit through praises, through tongues or through tears, then we can be free indeed from the fire of lust. As Jesus says, "I give you my assurance, everyone who lives in sin is the slave of sin. . . . That is why, if the Son frees you, you will really be free."

Anyone who has ever been a slave to sin knows how good it is finally to be set free by Christ! Are you still a slave to lust? Do you live in sexual immorality? Are your thoughts constantly dwelling on immoral sexual acts? Begin now to praise God. Let yourself cry. Let yourself praise God with sounds beyond human understanding. *Choose* to praise God, and feel His Spirit come upon you.

Then let that Spirit replace your impure thoughts with thoughts of God. Read the Scripture as you pray. Read it like a personal love letter from God. Read it as the divine plan for your life. Instead of trying to make the scriptures fit your way of life, conform your life to the way of the scripture. If you do this with the guidance of the Holy Spirit everyday, you will be set free.

Fiery Asceticism

To permanently overcome the fire of lust, however, we must do even more than just rely on the emotional experience of the Spirit. Sometimes the passion involved with what we perceive to be the Spirit can actually stir up the passion of lust in our souls all the more! True, the genuine passion of the Spirit evicts the passion of lust from our souls. But sometimes what we *think* is the Spirit, is really "an angel of darkness come as an angel of light." As St. John says, "Beloved, do not trust every spirit, but put the spirits to a test to see if they belong to God, because many false prophets have appeared in the world." We must not worship the charismatic gifts. We must worship the *Giver* of the gifts. Worship of the gift will only lead us headlong back into earthly passion.

Evagrius says, "Do not turn the very antidote of passion into passion. . . . This madness has led any number of persons astray. They have lost sight of the purpose of their tears even while weeping for their sins." We would do well to remember that a number of heretics have appeared to be highly charismatic and supposedly filled with the Spirit. The Montanists were charismatics, even though they claimed a higher authority for themselves than they gave to the Church, the scriptures, or even the apostles. The Cathari and the Spirituals of the Franciscan era did the same and often ended up leading lives of extreme sexual immorality, even ending the Mass with free and open sexual orgies around the altar. In our recent past, the tragedy of the Rev. Jim Jones and Jonestown reveals a similar journey with a tragic end. Numerous Christian communes have experienced the same thing to a lesser degree.

For the desert fathers, St. Francis, and all true charismatics of the Church, a healthy discipline and self-denial proved to be a further discipline in controlling the fire of lust. As we have already seen, the discipline of daily reading of scripture proves to be the safest way to fill our minds with the truth of God. But the scripture itself speaks of the self-denial and self-mastery of asceticism as a good practice when exercised properly.

St. Paul connects casting off sexual immorality and other sins to asceticism when he says, "Let us cast off the deeds of darkness and put on the armor of light. Let us live honorably as in daylight; not in carousing and drunkenness, not in sexual excess and lust. . . . Rather, put on the Lord Jesus Christ and make no provision for the desires of the flesh." He says again, "You know that while all the runners in the stadium take part in the race, the award goes to one man. In that case, run so as to win! Athletes deny themselves all sorts of things. They do this to win a crown of leaves that withers, but we a crown that is imperishable. I do not run like a man who loses sight of the finish line. . . . What I do is discipline my own body and master it, for fear that after having preached to others I myself should be rejected."

Jesus Himself does not question the need for certain ascetical practices. He does not say "*If* you fast"; He says, "*When* you fast, you are not to look glum as the hypocrites do." He says of some demons, "This kind you can only drive out by prayer and fasting." He Himself did battle with the devil during His forty-day fast in the desert.

The early Christian ascetics believed that all vices were interconnected. If you gave in to one vice, another would follow along soon. It was a kind of domino effect where if you knocked one down they would all fall down. In this thinking, if you gave in to speaking too often, silliness, coarse jesting and cursing were sure to follow. If you gave in to overeating, the body would be roused and sexual lust would follow. They called each vice according to its spiritual origin. Thus, they would speak of the demon of gluttony or the demon of fornication. These two demons, they said, were closely connected. These early desert fathers can sometimes seem outdated, but a careful reading of their understanding of the working of the human mind reveals that they possessed a wisdom gained through lived experience, not just from books.

Evagrius speaks of eight principal demons, each following more or less in succession: gluttony, impurity, avarice, sadness, anger, acedia—the noonday demon—vainglory, and pride. Of sexual sins he says, "The demon of impurity impels one to lust after bodies. It attacks more strenuously those who practice continence. Reading, vigils and prayer—these are the things that lend stability to the wandering mind. Hunger, toil and solitude are the means of extinguishing the flames of desire."

St. Maximus says similarly, "Certain things put a stop to movements of passion . . . others lessen them and make them decrease. For example, fasting, work, and vigils do not permit concupiscence to grow; while solitude and meditation, prayer and burning love for God diminish it and bring it to nothing." He continues,

The Fire of Lust

"All impassioned thoughts either excite the concupiscible, or stir up the irascible, or darken the rational element of the soul. Hence it comes that the mind is hampered in its spiritual contemplation .... [The monk and the solitary] should know this, for example: impassioned memories of women excite the soul's concupiscible element: their cause is want of self-control in eating and drinking and frequent, unreasonable association with these same women; hunger, thirst, vigils, and solitude cut them off." Francis of Assisi was also "convinced that it was dangerous to allow any representation of them to enter one's mind because the flame of passion could easily be rekindled."

St. Francis drew greatly from this ascetical tradition of the desert fathers. St. Bonaventure writes of him, "He used to say that it was hard to satisfy one's material needs without giving in to the inclinations of sensuality. As long as he enjoyed good health, he scarcely ever ate cooked food. When he did he mixed it with ashes or destroyed its taste, usually by adding water. He never drank enough water, even when he was burning with thirst—not to mention taking wine." As to protecting himself from the elements, he said, "If we are on fire with longing for our heavenly home in our hearts, we will have no difficulty in enduring exterior cold." As to fine clothing: "He knew from his own experience that the devils were afraid when they saw a person wearing rough clothes, whereas soft or luxurious garments gave them courage to attack all the more." Francis disciplined his sleep habits so that he did not sleep too long, nor would he allow himself too much comfort in sleep.

The logic is clear. If you have trouble with overeating, don't go to a place where too much food is readily available. If you can't stop overeating, fast completely. This will break your habit and silence your appetite. If you are fasting, it is not necessarily good to be around food. The same holds true for association with men or women and various sexual sins. As Jesus says, "Anyone who looks lustfully at a woman has already committed adultery with her in his thoughts. If your right eye is your trouble, gouge it out and

49

throw it away. . . . Again, if your right hand is your trouble, cut it off and throw it away! Better to lose part of your body than to have it cast into Gehenna."

Many people complain about this whole line of thinking. They say that these ascetics deny the goodness of the world that God created. It is a valid concern, and sometimes they are right. St. Paul does say, "In later times some will turn away from the faith and will heed deceitful spirits and things taught by demons through plausible liars [men with scared consciences] who forbid marriage and require abstinence from foods which God created to be received with thanksgiving by believers who know the truth. Everything God created is good; nothing is to be rejected when it is received with thanksgiving, for it is made holy by God's word and by prayer."

But Christian ascetics practice discipline precisely because they know of its goodness and value! For the Christian ascetic, the created world is interconnected in Christ. The physical world is connected to and affects the spiritual world just as the spiritual world is connected to and affects the physical world. Furthermore, they see virtue and vice linked together as a chain stretched out before a mirror. For every vice there is an opposite virtue, and for every virtue a vice. Sinning in one area against virtue opens the door not only to the opposite vice but to everything connected to it. This downward spiral is stopped by virtue in thought and action, which reverses the spiral and takes both body and soul to heaven. All of this is a very mystical and wholistic approach to the created world. But it does not deny creation's value. It affirms it!

St. Francis also affirmed the goodness of the created world, praising God for and through the wonders of creation. This is seen especially in his beautiful "Canticle of the Creatures." Francis's balance of the use of the creation is brought out by St. Bonaventure's account: "In everything beautiful he saw him who is beauty itself, and he followed his Beloved everywhere by his likeness imprinted on creation; of all creation he made a ladder by which he might mount up and embrace Him who is all desirable." Thomas of Celano's version brings out a healthy incarnational approach to use of the created world for asceticism: "Hurrying to leave this world inasmuch as it is the place of exile of our pilgrimage, this blessed traveler was yet helped not a little by the things that are in the world. With respect to the world 'rulers of this darkness' (Eph. 5:12), he used it as a field of battle; with respect to God, he used it as a very bright 'image of his goodness'" (Wis. 7:26).

Another problem with this kind of strict asceticism is that it can cause "demon paranoia" and unhealthy "hangups" about the body. We begin spending so much time thinking about demons and sin that they actually take hold more strongly in our lives. We think we are free, but we are still in their grip!

Maximus says much about guarding our thoughts in battling demons, but he also says the truly advanced monk will finally be able to "look with detachment when forms of women arise in the mind. . . . He who is perfect in love and has attained the summit of detachment knows no difference between 'mine and thine,' between faithful and unfaithful, between slave and freeman, or indeed between male and female."

Francis also finally approached the devil with a healthy detachment. He said to one after numerous battles, "On the part of Almighty God, I say to you, devils, do with my body whatever is granted you to do with it." Confronted with his passive trust in God, they "departed confused and in shame." Likewise we should never become so paranoid about devils that we lose our childlike innocence and joy. St. Francis maintained that the safest remedy against the thousand snares and wiles of the enemy is spiritual joy.

Our asceticism should exist only to lift our minds to God. If it draws us back to the things of the earth by concentrating too much energy and thought on the body, or even demons, it has defeated its very purpose. The fire of the ascetical life should exist only to lift our mind and body to the fire of God.

All that has been said here concerning the fire of lust also applies to other sins mentioned in this book. The fire of lust, the fire of anger, and the fire of the tongue are all combated in a similar way.

The Fire of God

Any sin that affects the mind and body can be overcome through praise, tongues, tears, and a healthy asceticism. In all of these things it is the fire of the Holy Spirit that must replace the particular fire of sin.

I recommend a healthy, balanced asceticism for those who seek to be free of their enslavement to lust and passions. It is a good idea to fast once a week. I recommend a substantial fast on bread and water, or fruit juice, if you are healthy enough to do so. Likewise, it is good to discipline your sleeping habits to about six to eight hours so that you do not give full rein to your desire for comfort and ease. If I give my body full rein in this area, it will want it in another area as well. Once a week, however, I suggest "sleeping in" for however short or long your body needs. I also recommend spending time in solitude and silence to avoid undue attachment to particular people or things. When this detachment is present, then occasional social activity is really more enjoyable.

I, and many others, have found these and similar ways to practice a healthy asceticism in today's world helpful. The simple discipline of turning off a TV movie that borders on the salacious helps my chastity immensely. I just don't need to fill my mind with such images. The same holds true for suggestive lyrics in a song over the radio. Remember: "Garbage in, garbage out." It is far better to take the time to praise God through praying or singing. And you will find this a lot more refreshing.

All of these things become healthy ways to use the very things of creation, but we must be properly detached. It is when we grow attached that the fire of lust grows in our souls. When this fire is in full flame, it destroys both our souls and the created world. The fire of the Spirit, however, glows like the burning bush on Sinai. It does not consume. It brings salvation!

Human Intimacy

All human beings have a need for intimacy. When God created us He said, "It is not good for the man to be alone. I will make a suitable partner for him." Ever since the beginning of the human race, human beings have sought intimacy with other human beings. This intimacy God speaks of is sexual. Usually it involves the genital sexuality of intercourse. This is not only normal, it is healthy and good. It is the way God created us.

As we consider the asceticism of dealing with the fire of lust, it is good to remember the value of human intimacy. Too often our attempts to guard our marital or celibate chastity have turned into paranoid hangups about "particular friendships" or innocent and healthy human contact. The stories of the extremes taken in religious houses to avoid either heterosexual or homosexual contact border on the absurd. Instead of nurturing a healthy chastity among the faithful, these attitudes and practices gave birth to a scrupulosity and paranoia that betrayed the life-style portrayed in the gospels of Jesus Christ. These extremes did not minister new life. They ministered death.

It is like trying to dam up the natural flow of a river. A dam can be a good thing. It can store up water for times of drought, and it can redirect the flow of the river more adequately to supply for human needs for miles around. But if you totally stop the natural flow of water you are in for big trouble! Eventually the water will build up too high behind the dam. The pressure on the dam will increase until finally the dam breaks in an unhealthy outburst of destructive power. Life will be swept away before the wall of uncontrolled water. It will destroy both the dam and the towns that lie in its runaway path.

So it is with human sexuality. Christian sexuality is more than just a stamp of approval on the fallen natural order. If this were true, all forms of sexual immorality would be acceptable options for the Christian. They are all evidenced throughout nature. Yet as it stands, they are not acceptable for us. We must let the fire of

53

God control our animal instincts and help raise sexuality to a new and higher level of spirituality. But if our sexuality is denied altogether, we create more problems than we solve. If we deny either the heterosexual or the homosexual inclinations and needs that live within us all, they will burst the dam of Church law with a destructive force that will be virtually unstoppable!

Scripture speaks of both heterosexual and homosexual relationships that are holy and good. It never, however, speaks of promiscuous sexual behavior of any sort as good.

Obviously, the marital relationship between a man and a woman is blessed by God. Jesus says, "Have you not read that at the beginning the Creator made them male and female and declared, 'For this reason a man shall leave his father and mother and cling to his wife, and the two shall become as one?' Thus they are no longer two but one flesh. Therefore, let no man separate what God has joined." He blessed sex saying, "Be fertile and multiply." St. Paul said explicitly, "The husband should fulfill his conjugal obligations toward his wife, and the wife hers toward her husband. . . . Do not deprive one another, unless perhaps by mutual consent for a time, to devote yourselves to prayer. Then return to one another, that Satan may not tempt you through your lack of self-control."

God even blessed nongenital homosexual love as long as it did not stir up homosexual temptation and lust. A legitimate love shared between close friends of the same sex is to be treasured.

This kind of love is spoken of between David and Jonathan. The scriptures say, "Jonathan had become as fond of David as if his life depended on him; he loved him as he loved himself. . . . And Jonathan entered into a bond with David, because he loved him as himself." Some have tried to say Jonathan and David were homosexual lovers, but the scriptures do not support this. They speak only of an intimate love between two very close friends. Their love was as selfless as the ideal love between a husband and wife. Paul says, "Each one should love his wife as he loves himself." This kind of love is to be shared by all people as part of the two great commandments of Jesus: "Love your neighbor as yourself." The scripture supports and puts value on a fond and beautiful love relationship between friends.

There is also scriptural evidence of physical expressions of this nonmarital love. In Paul's letters to the Romans, the Corinthians, the Thessalonians, and in Peter's first epistle, greeting one another with a "holy kiss" is mentioned. At the Last Supper "the disciple whom Jesus loved" unhesitantly and unashamedly "leaned back against Jesus' chest" to speak to Him. Apparently in Jesus' culture and time such expressions of love and closeness were perfectly accepted and encouraged. Even today you can see those of the same sex walking hand in hand or arm in arm through the streets of Jerusalem. It is not seen as "homosexual." It is seen as an expression of authentic love.

Even with St. Francis, who so scrupulously guarded against entering into relationships that might lead to a fall or to scandal, we see evidence of free and healthy manifestations of love between the Brothers and the Sisters of his Order. In his *Form of Life and Last Will for St. Clare,* he expresses his love for her: "I desire and promise you personally and in the name of my friars that I will always have the same loving care and special solicitude for you as for them."

The *Little Flowers* show that Francis sometimes eased his strict rule against familiarity with women. "When St. Francis was staying in Assisi, he often visited St. Clare and consoled her with holy advice. And as she had a very great desire to eat a meal with him once more, she asked him several times to give her that consolation. But St. Francis always refused to grant her that consolation. So it happened that his companions, perceiving St. Clare's desire, said to St. Francis, 'Father, it seems to us that this strictness is not according to divine charity.' Francis went on to bend his own rules and arranged to share a meal with Clare. During the meal, Francis and his companion, and Clare and her companion, paused to talk about God. Francis began this holy discussion and all were rapt in God by the overabundance of divine grace that descended upon them. And while they were sitting there, in a rapture, with their eyes and hands raised to Heaven, it seemed to the men of Assisi. . . that the forest which was at that time around the Place was all aflame and that an immense fire was burning over all of them."

Here the fire of lust was replaced with a holy fire of love. Instead of Francis and Clare getting together for romantic reasons, they gathered to share the table of friends and to discuss God, the Bridegroom of the Bride of Christ! Because of this a fire a thousand times more powerful than the power of lust was ignited. It was the fire of God's holy and pure love!

Jesus Himself leaves us with the example of men and women traveling and ministering together. They were not all married to one another, yet it never seemed to be a problem to Jesus. Luke's gospel says, "After this he journeyed through towns and villages preaching and proclaiming the good news of the kingdom of God. The Twelve accompanied him, and also some women who had been cured of evil spirits and maladies. . . and many others who were assisting them out of their means."

A healthy interreaction needs to take place between those of the opposite sex even though not married. To stifle these spiritual friendships will only hinder the natural desire placed within us by God. Often the stifling of healthy friendships outside of marriage will result only in eventual unhealthy expressions, in sexual sin. This is true in both celibate and married expressions of the love between friends.

Francis also fosters a healthy love between the Brothers. First he speaks of a healthy balance between the male and female dimensions in each of our personalities and the need to express them both. Thomas of Celano says, "It was always Francis's anxious wish and careful watchfulness to preserve among his sons the bond of unity, so that those whom the same Spirit drew together and the same father brought forth might be nurtured peacefully in the bosom of one mother." It is common knowledge that Francis spoke of the leaders of the fraternity as both spiritual fathers and mothers of their many sons. This is not some kind of weird new idea. It is based squarely on the example of St. Paul, and is used only to bring out both the strength and the tenderness needed in the good leader. Paul does call himself both father and mother to the communities he birthed in Christ.

Physical expressions of love also took place among the first friars that were not considered at all out of place. Thomas of Celano says, "Wherever they came together anywhere, or met one another along the way, as the custom is, there a shoot of spiritual love sprang up, sprinkling over all the seed of true affection. What more shall I say? Chaste embraces, gentle feelings, a holy kiss, pleasing conversation, modest laughter, joyous looks, a single eye. . . all these were found in them."

All of this means there can be healthy and holy expressions of human intimacy both inside and outside of marriage. Marriage alone allows for the genital expression of our sexuality, but legitimate hetero and homosexual expressions can, and even should, take place between spiritual friends.

But a word of warning needs to be added here: Many holy spiritual friends have ended up as unholy lovers by being too free with their expressions of affection. Ministers have ended up making love with the very people who come to them for counsel. Celibate Brothers and Sisters have found themselves burning with lust for one another during a "prayer session" or "spiritual encounter."

We should not think ourselves stronger than we really are. All of our freedom in these areas should always be seen against the backdrop of due discretion. And the asceticism of the ancients should not be too quickly discarded in order to embrace the so-called freedom of the "new age."

The Value of Celibate Love

Jesus says, "Some there are who have freely renounced sex for the sake of God's reign. Let him accept this teaching who can." He indicates that this is not for all His followers. Some, however, will feel called to follow Jesus' literal example in the area of celibacy. As Paul says, "A man is better off having no relations with a woman . . . . Given my preference, I should like you to be as I am. Still, each one has his own gift from God. . . . To sum up: the man who marries acts fittingly; the one who does not, will do better."

Celibacy is a sacrifice. You do not cease having sexual desires just because you have taken a vow. But you do sacrifice your desire for human sexual fulfillment in order to lead others to ultimate fulfillment in Christ. Likewise, you even give up the nongenital relationships that can lead into spiritual adultery. A celibate is literally married to Christ. Any romantic relationship that takes the place of our spiritual marriage becomes adultery. This means that those of us who have chosen celibacy must be very careful about the "spiritual friendships" we engage in. Some are good and healthy. Others are spiritual adultery. There might not be any sexual activity in the relationship, but the romantic fantasies of the relationship will cause us to commit adultery in our hearts.

Cajetan Esser, the late Franciscan scholar, says, "The distinctive character of the sexes and their consequent relationship to each other penetrates the whole compass of human existence. . . . This supposes and demands, on both planes, the power of mutual attraction. On the higher level this is usually called Eros, in distinction to sex. Sex seeks the bodily or physical union and complement; Eros, the spiritual perfection of the partners. . . . The man (or woman) who consecrates himself to virginity renounces both aspects of marriage. Not only does he give up the exercise of his power of sex and all right to earthly progeny, but also sacrifices the fulfillment in Eros of his soul's desire. The 'life of chastity' therefore cannot and does not reach its full meaning only on the level of sexual continence, that is, of mere bodily chastity. This would be only half a sacrifice."

Esser goes on to point out the need of a positive fulfillment in Christ to see us through this sacrifice. Otherwise we begin to fill up our emptiness with various "spiritual adulteries" even in the name of Christ. He says, "Such flights from the heights where all

belongs to God and nothing to self can take many forms: work and feverish activity, into which one plunges to drown out the cries of the heart; the enjoyment of the abundant life in one way or the other, in good food and drink, amusements, distractions, as a false recompense for the sacrifice one has made. A more frequent form is found in a masked sensuality, particularly in the form of would-be spiritual friendships with the opposite sex. In like manner, a certain craving for the security and heartwarming atmosphere of the family and the home must be considered as hurtful to the vow of chastity and a failing against it."

I have experienced most of these things in my own life as a celibate. Often I will find myself attracted to a particular Sister. Soon I find that I want to be around her a lot, not so much for spiritual friendship, but to fill the void I have from not being married. I don't really want a sexual encounter, but I do want the companionship I miss from marriage. But only Jesus can fill that void for me now. When I seek its filling by another human being, I am not really entering into the fullness of my vow of chastity in a positive way. I am still holding back on fully embracing Jesus as the Bridegroom of my soul.

Likewise, sometimes I seek small but habitual sense gratifications from so-called spiritual friends. It is good to show affection. We need it. But when I begin to need habitual shows of affection from one particular person, I am usually in trouble. The need always to be around someone, or hug them, or get my "stiff neck" rubbed by them are all ways this has surfaced in my life. These signs of affection might be innocent in themselves, but interiorly they are only incomplete attempts at fulfilling a misguided search for romantic sexual love.

Perhaps I sound foolish in exposing my own experience here. But it has also been my experience that I am not alone. Many of my Brothers and Sisters vowed to chastity are only incompletely fulfilling their vow. Externally we are all right. No gross sexual sins have been committed. But interiorly we are often in habitual sins of spiritual adultery.

The Fire of God

All of this is like the analogy of fire. In and of itself fire is a good thing. When we light a fire in our fireplace, it brings light and warmth into our house. But if a log rolls out of the fireplace onto the living-room floor, it could burn down the whole house. The fire that spreads outside of the fireplace becomes a destructive thing. Left within the fireplace, it remains positive and good. Sometimes, it is a good idea to put up supports and fireguards to keep the fire and the wood within the fireplace of our house.

So it is with human intimacy. If the fire of mutual human attraction is a controlled fire within the fireplace of God's order, it brings health and goodness to all. If our relationships get out of control and burn outside of God's will and order, they become destructive for all those involved. The need for human intimacy needs to be controlled by the will of God. Likewise, a healthy discipline or asceticism helps to control this fire of human love.

Finally, the need for intimacy between people should lead us to, and cause us to be fulfilled in, God. As St. Bonaventure says, "The created universe itself is a ladder leading us toward God. . . . The creatures of this sensible world signify the invisible attributes of God." Even in our temptations we should thank God for giving us reminders that He, and He alone can be the Bridegroom of our soul. Even our sexual temptations then become reminders of spiritual sexuality that is fulfilled between God and His people. Thus, our eternal sexuality is totally fulfilled only in Him who is eternal. Our need for intimacy and friendship is fulfilled only in Him who is most intimate. I will not repeat here what I have already treated at length in my book, *The Lover and the Beloved*, but I will leave you with a thought I wrote about Francis. "No human tongue could describe the passionate love with which Francis burned for Christ, His Spouse; he seemed to be completely absorbed by the fire of divine love like a glowing coal. . . . The fire of divine love burned the more perfectly in his heart for all that it only became clearly visible in his flesh later on in life." This, of course, is an allusion to the stigmata where his love relationship with Jesus was finally and fully consummated.

From Francis himself: "On all those who do this and endure to the last the Spirit of God will rest. . . . It is they who are the brides, the brothers and the mothers of our Lord Jesus Christ. A person is his bride when his faithful soul is united with Jesus Christ by the Holy Spirit; we are his brothers when we do the will of His Father who is in heaven (Matt. 12:50), and we are mothers to Him when we enthrone Him in our hearts and souls by love with a pure sincere conscience, and give birth to Him by doing good."

Such intimacy can only be symbolized by two people on earth and shared in part. God is the only one who can fully satisfy our natural desire for intimacy. He created us in His image. Our desire for human intimacy is a reflection of a divine reality. He created us with the desire for intimacy. But He is the only one who can completely fulfill it.

4
The Fire of Anger

Anger is another of the most destructive fires. It is one that seethes within the human heart. It starts out with a small spark of resentment, but when it is fanned with the sin of judgment it develops into a full flame. This flame can burn through a person's whole life. It will affect every thought, every word, and every action. It will affect every relationship. The fire of anger will spread through a person's whole life, destroying everything in its path. In the end all that will be left is despair. This, in turn, will finally lead a person to death.

Our old friend, Evagrius Ponticus, also has much to say about anger. "The most fierce passion is anger. In fact it is defined as a boiling and stirring up of wrath against one who has injury—or is thought to have done so. It constantly irritates the soul and above all at the time of prayer it seizes the mind and flashes the picture of the offensive person before one's eyes. Then there comes a time when it persists longer, is transformed into indignation, stirs up alarming experiences at night. This is succeeded by a general debility of the body . . . and the illusion of being attacked."

Basically, anger is no fun. It is not fun to be angry. It just doesn't feel good. Most people I know who are angry don't really enjoy it. I don't enjoy it when I am angry! It churns us up inside. It makes us sick. It makes us defensive in all our relationships. We really aren't fun to be around either. Anger is no fun for anybody!

Jesus brings out the interconnectedness of anger with other sins. He actually links anger with murder! He says, "You have heard the commandment imposed on your forefathers, 'You shall not murder; every murderer shall be liable to judgment.' What I say to you is: everyone who grows angry with his brother shall be liable to judgment; any man who uses abusive language toward his brother shall be answerable to the Sanhedrin, and if he holds him in contempt he risks the fires of Gehenna." Here, again, the anger ends in a fire of destruction when it has run its course.

The Fire of God

Dietrich Bonhoeffer, the acclaimed Lutheran theologian who lost his life during the Nazi persecution, says in his book *The Cost of Discipleship*, "Anger is always an attack on the brother's life, for it refuses to let him live and aims at his destruction. . . . The angry word is a blow struck at our brother, a stab at his heart: it seeks to hit, to hurt and destroy." For this theologian and martyr, anger toward another is equal in seriousness to murder.

St. Paul implies the same thing by including both murder and anger in his list of sins of the flesh: "It obviously proceeds from the flesh: lewd conduct, impurity, licentiousness, idolatry, sorcery, hostilities, bickering, jealousy, outbursts of rage, selfish rivalries, dissensions, factions, envy, drunkenness, orgies, and the like. I warn you, as I have warned you before: those who do such things will not inherit the kingdom of God."

It is amazing how interwoven all these things are. Sometimes we think small things are not important, but they are. Be it virtue or vice, small things are just as important as the things we perceive as big and important. But big things grow from small things. Actions grow from feelings. And feelings are guided by thoughts. Because of this anger can be seen as just as destructive as murder itself.

Maximus says the same: "Self-love, as we have often said, is the cause of all the impassioned thoughts. By it are begotten the three capital thoughts of concupiscence—gluttony, avarice, and vainglory. By gluttony fornication of thought is begotten; by avarice, rapacity of thought; by vainglory, pride of thought. All the rest follow one or the other of these three—the thoughts of anger, grief, grudges, sloth, envy, detraction and the rest."

James speaks of another kind of murder: "Where do conflicts and disputes among you originate? Is it not your inner cravings that make war within your members? What you desire you do not obtain, and so you resort to murder."

This kind of anger occurs when we have not really detached ourselves from our possessions. These possessions may be anything. They could be external or internal. They could be our ideas or our values, as well as our external possessions. As soon as someone tries to take or destroy one of these possessions we grow defensive and angry. Someone disagrees with our opinion and we grow angry. Someone takes what we think is ours and we do the same.

St. Francis speaks of the connection between anger and poverty of spirit in his fourteenth admonition. "There are many people who spend all their time at their prayers and other religious exercises and mortify themselves by long fasts and so on. But if anyone says as much as a word that implies a reflection on their self-esteem or takes something from them, they are immediately up in arms and annoyed. These people are not really poor in spirit. A person is poor in spirit when he hates himself and loves those who strike him in the face (Matt. 5:39)."

Jesus teaches a radical approach to both poverty and nonresistance. This nonresistance is possible only because there is no anger. There can be no anger when we have given up all our possessions. This is why Jesus says, "You have heard the commandment, 'An eye for an eye, a tooth for a tooth.' But what I say to you is: offer no resistance to injury. When a person strikes you on the right cheek, turn and offer him the other. If anyone wants to go to law over your shirt, hand him your coat as well. Should anyone press you into service for one mile, go with him two miles."

We are not talking about little day-in-and-day-out things here. We're talking about major attacks! To be hit. To be sued. These are all things that would make most of us very angry. No one would blame us if we fought back. But Jesus commands us not to. Jesus can give us this command because He can deal with the cause of war. He can deal with our anger and our hatred. But it is not enough just to repress our anger. We must replace it with something better!

The Fire of Love

Jesus continues: "You have heard the commandment: 'You shall love your countrymen but hate your enemy.' My command to you is: love your enemies, pray for your persecutors. . . . If you love those who love you, what merit is there in that? Do not tax collectors do as much? And if you greet your brothers only, what is so praiseworthy about that? Do not pagans do as much?"

Jesus calls us to love actively those who make us angry. This kind of love is not only an emotion. It is a choice. Our emotions usually lead us to anger, hatred, and war. If we really want peace we must first choose to love even when our emotions tend toward anger. This is not easy. It takes much discipline and much time to be substantially free of our response of anger to an affront of any kind. As we have already said, the mind directs the feelings, and sinful actions come forth from our emotions. Thus, there is a definite connection between our thoughts and our emotions. These two then work together in controlling our actions.

If we have trouble with anger, we must begin filling our mind with something better. We must choose to fill it with love! Jesus says, "pray for your persecutors." This means we must begin making a conscious effort with our mind to love and make peace with our enemies. This involves some creative visualizing. I recommend taking time every day to meditate. Using the teachings of Jesus Christ, intentionally direct your thoughts to pray for your enemy's genuine well-being. This does not mean some kind of patronizing prayer to "cover your bases" before you let them have it with "justice." It means a genuine prayer for their well-being.

If you do this, you will slowly find your anger changing into love. If you will take the time really to pray for a person, you will begin to feel closer to them. You will begin to see things a little more from their perspective. You can no longer really wish for their harm. You can only desire their well-being and good. Your anger is being transformed by love.

But even this won't succeed if you still hold onto your possessions. You will love them only until they jeopardize your control or use of what you consider "yours." This means you will again be defensive, and it will eventually lead you to anger once more. Therefore you must also meditate on yourself! You must visualize yourself living in gospel poverty. See yourself with nothing to defend. See yourself as a poor pilgrim wandering the earth in perfect peace and joy. See your hands open with nothing to possess, nothing to grasp, nothing to defend. Yet see yourself in total peace. Soon your anger will diminish even more in the light of embracing the poverty of Christ.

This is really a meditation on sharing the cross of Jesus. On the cross we are naked and poor. On the cross even our life is abandoned. All is at peace. All is at rest. Yet in this peace and rest we find new life. From the cross we find resurrection.

Francis suggests a similar meditation: "Take a lifeless body and place it where you will. You will see that it does not resist being moved, it does not murmur about its position, it does not cry out." St. Paul suggests a similar focusing when discussing being free of the life of vice and living a life of virtue. "Be intent on things above rather than on things of earth. After all, you have died. . . . Put to death whatever in your nature is rooted in earth. . . . You must put all that aside now: all the anger and quick temper, the malice, the insults. . . . What you have done is put aside your old self with its past deeds and put on the new man . . . formed anew in the image of his Creator."

But there is another kind of anger. It is the anger caused by the sins or idiosyncrasies of those around us. These things are not necessarily affronts directed at us personally. They are the things that go on around us . . . the little things and sins that occur day after day. These are the things that can drive us absolutely crazy.

St. Francis speaks of this kind of anger: "All the friars . . . should be careful not to be upset or angry when anyone falls into sin or gives bad example; the devil would be only too glad to ensnare many others through one man's sin. They are bound, on the contrary, to give the sinner spiritual aid, as best they can."

Most of the time it is not some big issue that makes us angry. Usually it is some little something that really gets under our skin. It is usually something very insignificant done by somebody very close to us. It is usually done by those we live with. It could be your family or your community. It is usually someone whom you really care for very much, but for some reason something about them begins to drive you crazy.

These kinds of things have a way of building in our mind. Little thing after little thing occurs. The fire of anger is ignited. Soon we begin to stew inside. Then we begin actually looking for the things the other person or persons is doing wrong. Then we really begin to boil. Usually nothing or very little is being done wrong. It is only our anger that has blown the little failings of someone else way out of proportion. Literally, our anger has a way of making "mountains out of molehills." It is only by getting rid of this anger that we can peacefully deal with molehills as molehills, rather than with the dynamite sometimes needed to blast away a mountain.

Thanksgiving

I have found that the only way to combat this anger is through thanksgiving. It is an intentional choice to look for the good points in the person driving you crazy and actively to thank God for them! By doing this you will slowly begin to reappreciate their good points so that the bad ones no longer seem so bad. It will not make the bad ones go away, but it will bring them back into perspective so that they can be dealt with without anger. Once you begin to dwell on the bad, your anger will only get worse. Once you dwell primarily on the good, the bad can be dealt with without anger. St. Paul speaks of this when he says, "Dedicate yourselves to thankfulness."

But Paul also speaks of thanking God for all things. As we have seen in dealing with the fire of lust, Paul says, "Give thanks to God the Father always and for everything." It is not enough to thank

God only for a person's good points. You must actually thank God for the very thing that is making you angry! It is this very thing that is given to us by God through them to help us overcome anger. It is a gift to us. It is not our enemy. It is our friend. It is only by thanking God for the very things that make us angry that we will be free of our anger. It sounds silly, but it is true.

St. Francis speaks of the principle of thanking God in all things when he encourages those who are sick. "I beg the friar who is sick to thank God for everything; he should be content to be as God wishes him to be, in sickness or in health, because . . . God instructs in sickness and affliction and the spirit of compunction."

St. Maximus encourages thankfulness in and for trial and tribulation as well: "The prudent man . . . thankfully bears the misfortunes that come upon him." But we cannot thank God for trial and tribulation if we don't believe there is a final reason for them being present in our life. Concerning the final reason for battle with the demon of anger, or any other demon, St. Maximus says, "There are five reasons, they say, why God permits us to be warred upon by the demons. (1) that in the attacks and counterattacks we come to distinguish virtue and vice; (2) that possessing virtue in such combat struggle, we shall hold it firm and steadfast; (3) that with advance in virtue we do not become high-minded but learn to be humble; (4) that having had some experience of vice, we will hate it with consummate hate; and (5) above all that when we become detached we forget not our own weakness nor the power of Him who has helped us." Here we can thank God for our anger because it actually leads us beyond anger to an experience of God's love that is humble and good.

Evagrius also says, "Anger is given to us so that we might fight against the demons and strive against every pleasure." He assumes correctly that we will win. St. John says, "Greater is he who is in you than he who is in the world."

Yet even with all these helps, sometimes it is impossible to break free of anger. Its fire burns within our deepest soul. Somehow it is more than the particular person or action. This anger actually abides within us. Its flames burn hot and they burn deep. We throw water on the flames continually, but the fire will not go out. Try as we may, the anger abides and its fire burns deep in our soul slowly to destroy our whole life!

This kind of anger is not a particular anger. It is an attitude of anger that abides with us constantly. This kind of anger is usually traceable to a particular situation where we were deeply offended or hurt by another person, or even a circumstance. It resulted in an anger directed toward a person, or even toward God for allowing the circumstance.

Instead of being reconciled in this situation with the person or with God, we stored up this anger and resentment deep in our souls. There it began to fester like a splinter that had yet to be removed. The infection grew worse and worse and began to spread to everything it touched. Consequently, more and more situations occurred that made us angry. The anger affected every new situation, and every new situation that did not go exactly as we wanted made us more angry. This anger began snowballing through our life, becoming larger and larger with each new situation. Left unchecked, this anger will destroy our whole life as it finally collides at the end of its runaway course with an immovable object . . . God.

Forgiveness

The only way to stop this kind of anger is through forgiveness and reconciliation. Jesus says, "Bring your gift to the altar and if you recall that your brother has anything against you, leave your gift at the altar, go first to be reconciled with your brother, and then come offer your gift." Paul says also, "The sun must not go down on your wrath; do not give the devil a chance to work on you." James says, "Hence, declare your sins to one another, and pray for one another, that you may find healing."

We must not only do this with our present situations, we must also do it with our past. Our very memories must be healed. Jesus says, "If you recall that your brother has anything against you." So often we try not to deal with the hurts and resentments of our past. We bury our anger deeper and deeper until it finally bursts forth in full outrage. It is like pushing a spring down tighter and tighter until, one day, it finally releases. When it does, it will be with full force. The same thing is true when we try to ignore the anger and resentments of our past. We must face our demon of anger if we are to conquer it.

For this I suggest what is called the "healing of memories." In this process an individual goes back to these angers under the guidance of a qualified counselor or spiritual director. It can be dangerous if tried alone. With the help of his or her director the person goes back to a specific situation. He or she relives the incident that caused the anger, but this time the person chooses to forgive. Sometimes it might be necessary to forgive another. Sometimes the person might need to forgive himself or herself. Sometimes it might even seem to be necessary to forgive God! (Even though God didn't really sin.) The process opens the way to a realization that the person really needs self-forgiveness for not obeying or trusting God. In this forgiveness comes healing.

This process is gone through situation after situation. It is like peeling the skin off an onion. Situation after situation brings forgiveness after forgiveness. Tear after tear is shed, and sin after sin is cleansed. Slowly the core of the problem is revealed, where the individual began the whole futile journey of anger. After the core is truly forgiven, the individual is fully restored and healed.

Many times it is at this core that things are most difficult. It is relatively easy to forgive the many particular situations caused by the core problem. But the core problem is something we have subconsciously held onto for a long time. It has grown like an old friend in our souls. How would we live without it? It is like a little rock with which we have been weighted down. Instead of throwing it away, we have kept it. We have polished it as if it were a precious stone. We have even enshrined it to try and justify its presence in

71

our life. We have "possessed" the "rightness" of our "justified" anger for so long that it is very difficult actually to give up.

Many times it is almost impossible to bring ourselves to allow forgiveness to operate in this core situation. It might be a problem we had with our mother or father, brother or sister in the distant past. It might be a wound that left a scar deep in the soul. We have so enshrined it in our life that it is almost impossible to think of it as anything less than a god!

In these situations it is, indeed, difficult to bring ourselves to forgive someone for something we think is so obviously wrong. Likewise, we might find it even more difficult actually to forgive ourselves. Try as we may, we just can't bring ourselves to forgive anyone for those sins that are so deeply set in our soul with such anger and resentment. The same can hold true at the beginning of this process. We have grown so accustomed to responding in anger that we just can't break free. It is like an old habit that is next to impossible to break. We want to stop, but we just can't!

The Gift of Tongues

In both of these situations I have found the gift of tongues very helpful. Here again the fire of the Spirit alone can permanently free us of the habitual and deeply set fire of anger. We must often fight fire with fire! As Paul says, "The Spirit too helps us in our weakness . . . with groanings that cannot be expressed in speech . . . for we do not know how to pray as we should."

During these times we just cry out to God for help. We cannot formulate the words. Our minds are too clouded with anger. Our thoughts are too prone to judgment. In tongues we are able to let our deepest spirit be released from the prison of anger and resentment. The Spirit lifts our spirits from the depths of our souls, purifying our thoughts and our feelings as spirits rise to the surface.

Amazing as it might sound, praying in tongues is able to accomplish more than a hundred intense therapy sessions. With tongues, the spirit can break free. We are able to forgive with our spirit, even though the heart and mind are not yet able to face the reality of a particular situation. When the spirit is free, the heart and the mind will soon be able to follow.

That is why I suggest being open to the prayer of tongues whenever we are faced with healing our anger. What we can't yet face with our thoughts and feelings can be faced and dealt with by our spirit when united with His Spirit.

The scriptures also speak of a healthy anger. Paul says, "If you're angry, let it be without sin. The sun must not go down on your wrath." Jesus was, no doubt, angry when He overturned the moneychangers' tables in the temple. His disciples remembered the scripture, "Zeal for your house consumes me," when they saw His angry demonstration. God Himself is spoken of as angry and wrathful; yet we know that God is both good and loving.

As we have said, it is not good to repress anger and resentment. The more you repress it, the more destructive it will be when it finally reveals itself. It is like a powder keg waiting to go off. The more you repress it, the more dynamite you store within your heart. The more you repress it, the bigger the destructive fire of its inevitable explosion.

It is very important to be able to express your displeasure with a situation or person when they offend or frustrate you. It is important to communicate. This should not necessarily be done in anger. It should be done in love. Paul says, "Speak the truth in love." Is it true that you are offended? Then say so, but say so in love. Is it true you are angry? Then say so, but say so in love. It is very important to vent your feelings, but to do so in love.

In this circumstance you might even say you are angry and resentful, but that you don't necessarily want to be. You might say to your brother or your sister, "I don't really know if my feelings are right or wrong, but I do know they exist. You did upset me. Please let's talk about it so I can be free of my feelings." Nine times out of ten it is this open and honest dialogue that will see a person through to forgiveness and reconciliation.

It is important in this dialogue to avoid judgment. A person must have the freedom to state his feelings without fear. When feelings have been openly and honestly shared, then we can usually judge, forgive, and change ourselves in the appropriate areas. Likewise, such honest and mutually trusting sharings usually bring mutual forgiveness with relative ease.

It cannot be emphasized enough that the truth should be shared in love. This love means we must approach one another naked and poor. We cannot try to hang onto any of our "possessions." If we do, we will be forced to defend them. As soon as we try to defend our position, the old barriers will go back up, war will break out, and anger and resentment will only increase. When this happens, those times intended for reconciliation and healing will boomerang and bring only more fuel to feed the fire of anger, resentment, and hatred. Here we do well to remember the saying of St. James: "A man's anger does not fulfill God's justice." Let us share the truth of our feelings, but let us do so only after we have chosen to do it in mutual love.

There is also a healthy asceticism involved in cooling the heat of our anger. This asceticism is not so much used during or after we have already been angry. It is used before we become angry. It is a preventative medicine for anger, where everything else we have discussed is used to heal an anger that already is.

Maximus says, "For anger: long suffering, forgetfulness of grudges, and meekness put a stop to it and do not allow it to grow; while charity, alms, kindness, and benevolence make it diminish." This is somewhat preventative, but still deals after the fact. Evagrius simply warns, "Do not give yourself over to your angry thoughts so as to fight in your mind with the one who has vexed you . . . it invites to the burning of passion." He also speaks of cooling the heat of another's anger. "A gift snuffs out the fire of resentment, as Jacob well knew." This is nice, as far as it goes.

Patience and Humility

St. Francis speaks of the preventative medicine for anger in his twenty-seventh Admonition. His words speak simply but have vast ramifications. Their depth could easily be overlooked. "Where there is Patience and Humility, there is neither Anger nor Annoyance." His words speak of a positive asceticsm. They do not just say what to do when you are already angry. They say what to do to help prevent anger. This is an ongoing discipline that can help us from day to day as we look to the future. It is one thing to put a Band-Aid on a cut. It is quite another to learn how to avoid being cut. The asceticism of Francis teaches us how to prevent anger. It gets below anger's symptoms and prevents its actual cause.

But how do we live in patience and humility? As with any virtue, it is one thing to know what is right, and it is quite another to do it. The law itself is unable to save us. It is the Spirit's renewal of our mind that will fill us with the right emotions. The choice to be patient and humble will fill us with the goodness of these virtues as feelings. When these virtuous feelings habitually occupy our heart it will be very difficult for anger to find its home there again.

This also involves the discipline, or asceticism, of positive visualization. We must actually choose to fill our mind with concrete examples of patience and humility. This means habitually meditating on Jesus' example of all virtues that combat anger and resentment. Patience, humility, poverty, and forgiveness are all virtues that combat the fire of anger. We should constantly turn our minds to the example of Jesus as depicted in the gospels. This will help us immensely when we ourselves are faced with similar situations. It will help us to respond like Christ.

We should learn to see ourselves responding like Christ in concrete situations. See Jesus standing beside you, walking with you through situations, helping you in your weakness. Then see yourself alone in the same situation, responding with the strength of the Holy Spirit who dwells within.

As Boniface Maes says in his work *Franciscan Mysticism*, "Pro-

pose for our meditation concrete cases in which we will have to exercise such and such virtues. Thus, for the virtue of patience you
may represent to yourself what you would do if anyone would inflict on you any injury of which you feel a horror."

Most of us deal with thoughts like this. We think to ourselves
what we would do in this or that situation if so and so did this or
that to us. Left to ourselves we often see ourselves striking back
with a seemingly justified anger or victorious comment. This only
"programs" us to respond in exactly the same way when a similar
situation actually comes up. It programs us for anger.

If we practice the above meditation as an ascetical discipline, it
will program us for virtue. We will defeat anger by preventing it
with positive virtue. This is an ongoing discipline that involves
both scripture reading and intentional times of solitude and silence. It is a choice that dedicates us to the discipline of meditation
so that we might be freed from slavery to sin and anger.

I also think a daily time to pray intentionally in tongues helps to
prevent anger. There are many subconscious thoughts and judgments that can slowly build toward anger and resentment. Praying in the Spirit allows the spirit to deal with these things before
they even surface. Anger and resentment that cannot even be formulated in conscious thoughts or words are dealt with by the Spirit
who prays within us in a way beyond understanding or speech.
Things that lurk only as vague, undefined feelings can sometimes
be totally dealt with with a prayer that is not limited to logic. For
me this is most powerfully accomplished by the gift of tongues.

To conclude: It is only possible to meet the problems of war and
peace if we first deal with our own anger. We cannot expect really
to bring peace to the war-torn areas of the world unless we first bring
to peace the anger that rages in our own human heart. We think the
problem of the nuclear-arms race is very important to the Christian
conscience, and rightly so. But unless we deal with the anger that
builds up within our own hearts, we can never bring peace or justice to the world. The fire of the nuclear holocaust begins with the
fire of an angry human heart. You cannot prevent the one unless
you first heal and prevent the other.

5
The Fire of the Tongue

The tongue's fire carries great destructive power. It often speaks forth from the flames of lust and anger dwelling deep within us. The tongue puts these inner fires into action, spreading destruction to others. We spend much time speaking about the sins of nuclear war and injustice, but until we learn to tame our own tongues, all this effort will come to nothing. It is the tongue that gives the command to attack. The tongue can speak forth from the anger, resentment, and lust within both persons and entire nations. If we tame the fires of sin within the human heart, then we must also tame the tongue. If we say we have tamed the one without the other, we deceive ourselves. But if we can tame both heart and tongue, then we have won the greatest of all individual battles for world peace.

The scriptures speak clearly and at great length about the inflammatory power of the tongue. St. James compares it to the very fires of hell. He says. "See how tiny the spark is that sets a huge forest ablaze! The tongue is such a flame. It exists among our members as a whole universe of malice. The tongue defiles the entire body. Its flames encircle our course from birth, and its fire is kindled by hell."

Sirach says, "If you blow upon a spark, it quickens into flame; if you spit on it, it dies out; yet both you do with your mouth!" As James also says, "Blessing and curse come out of the same mouth. This ought not to be, my brothers!" Needless to say, the potential of the effect of the tongue is vast. It can do much good. It can also stir up entire nations to unrest and war.

Our words are the extension of our very souls. It is by our words that the reality of our souls is put into action. Jesus says, "The mouth speaks whatever fills the mind." Some versions say our words flow "out of the abundance of the heart." Jesus goes on to say it is not only by our actions but by our very words that we will be judged. "A good man produces good from his store of goodness; an evil man produces evil from his evil store. I assure you, on judgment day people will be held accountable for every unguarded word they speak. By your words you will be acquitted, and by your words you will be condemned."

Jesus brings out the connection between the words we speak and the condition of our mind and soul when He says, "Do you not see that everything that enters the mouth passes into the stomach and is discharged into the latrine, but what comes out of the mouth originates in the mind? It is things like these that make a man impure. From the mind stem evil designs—murder, adulterous conduct, fornication, stealing, false witness."

Jesus Himself is the ultimate example of the power of words. He is the very Word of the Father. He represents the very "soul" of God. His whole life is a divine Word. The Word is good because God is good. It is powerful because God is powerful. St. John says, "In the beginning was the Word; the Word was in God's presence, and the Word was God. . . . The Word became flesh and made his dwelling among us, and we have seen his glory, the glory of an only Son coming from the Father, filled with enduring love." This is why not accepting Jesus is so much more tragic than not accepting a holy man, a guru, or a teacher. Jesus is God's living Word! If you reject the Word of God, you reject God's very soul.

The connectedness between the soul and our words is brought out in Jesus' teaching on anger. He says, "Everyone who grows angry with his brother shall be liable to judgment." He then speaks about the next stage of the development of anger: "Any man who uses abusive language toward his brother shall be answerable to the Sanhedrin, and if he holds him in contempt he risks the fires of Gehenna." Some translations say that this "contempt" is in calling your brother a "fool." Again this is a sin of the tongue that leads to the fires of hell from which it comes.

The tongue also has the power to speak things into existence. This works both for good and for evil. Jesus says of the Church, "Whatever you declare bound on earth shall be held bound in heaven, and whatever you declare loosed on earth shall be held loosed in heaven." It is in speaking our faith that mountains are moved in prayer. It was the spoken word of Jesus' "I am he" which forced a whole cohort of armed guards to fall to the ground. It was Jesus' spoken word that both cursed the fig tree and healed many of those who approached Him. Even with ourselves, it is the spoken confession of our lips that solidifies our salvation. Paul says, "If you confess with your lips that Jesus is Lord, and believe in your heart that God raised him from the dead, you will be saved. Faith in the heart leads to justification, confession on the lips to salvation."

When we speak words, our feelings and thoughts are made flesh, or concretized. Through words, our feelings and thoughts become exposed for all to hear. They will not be quickly forgotten, no matter how foolish. What we feel must first be processed in our minds, and then what is in our minds flows forth into words. In this process our true feelings are clarified. Often when we say something we hear how silly it really sounds, and we must reassess it in our mind. Oftentimes mutual dialogue or group discussion aids in this process. Other times it is the speaking itself that clarifies and sets in firm place the real contents of our human souls. When this happens there is a sudden and unmistakable release of either good or bad spiritual power.

The book of Proverbs says, "Death and life are in the power of the tongue." The tongue can build or destroy friendships. It can either bring life to or kill even the best of human relationships. The book of Sirach speaks of the destructive power of harsh words between friends: "He who throws stones at birds drives them away, and he who insults a friend breaks up the friendship. Should you draw a sword against a friend, despair not, it can be undone. Should you speak sharply to a friend, fear not, you can be reconciled. But a contemptuous insult, a confidence broken . . . will drive away any friend."

We all know these "breakthrough" moments when the spoken word has communicated the true intent of the soul against a close friend. Maybe you have said nothing for years. You have only felt and thought. Then suddenly you speak. Your words are sharp and cut to the soul of your friend. You are aware that this power has gone out from you. You are immediately sorry, but it is too late. You have already spoken the thought into existence! In just a few words a relationship can be destroyed. Even after years, all it takes is a few words and the friendship is over. To reconcile it will take much more dialogue and action. Trust will have to be reestablished. You will have to start over from scratch.

The fire of sin is projected out to our brothers and sisters through the fire of the tongue. It destroys us as long as we keep it within. It destroys our brothers and sisters as soon as we speak it forth. This is why the theologian Dietrich Bonhoeffer says, "The angry word is a blow struck at our brother, a stab at his heart; it seeks to hit, to hurt, and to destroy."

Gossip and Slander

The main way this occurs is through gossip and slander. Proverbs says, "Like a crazed archer scattering firebrands and deadly arrows is the man who deceives his neighbor and then says, 'I was only joking.' For lack of wood, the fire dies out; and when there is no talebearer, strife subsides. What a bellows is to live coals, what wood is to fire, such is a contentious man in enkindling strife. The words of a talebearer are like dainty morsels that sink into one's inmost being." And Sirach says, "A quarrelsome man kindles disputes, commits the sin of disrupting friendships and sows discord among those at peace. The more wood, the greater the fire; the more underlying it, the fiercer the fight. . . . Pitch and resin makes fire flare up. . . . If you blow upon a spark, it quickens into flame . . . . Cursed be gossips and the double-tongued, for they destroy the peace of many. A meddlesome tongue subverts many, and makes them refugees among the peoples. It destroys walled cities, and overthrows powerful dynasties. A meddlesome tongue can drive virtuous women from their homes and rob them of the fruit of their toil. . . . A blow from a whip raises a welt, but a blow from the tongue smashes bones. Many have fallen by the edge of the sword, but not as many as by the tongue. . . . Dire is the death it inflicts." Such descriptive words for the destructive nature of the fire of the tongue can be found nowhere else in scripture. There is no question that we do well to try and stop the fire of nuclear war, but the fire of the human tongue can be just as destructive.

St. Paul speaks of the sins of the tongue in a similar way. "Get rid of all bitterness, all passion and anger, harsh words, slander, and malice of every kind. . . . Your own conduct was once of this sort, when these sins were your very life. You must put all that aside now: all the anger and quick temper, the malice, the insults, the foul language. Stop lying to one another." He says to Titus concerning the Church, "Tell them not to speak evil of anyone or be quarrelsome. They must be forbearing and display a perfect courtesy toward all." St. Peter also says, "He who cares for life and wants to see prosperous days must keep his tongue from evil and his lips from uttering deceit." But it is James who speaks the most clearly and clarifies the "bottom line" in all this: "Let every man be quick to hear, slow to speak, slow to anger, for a man's anger does not fulfill God's justice. . . . If a man who does not control his tongue imagines he is devout, he is self-deceived; his worship is pointless." This is why Paul includes slander and gossip in his list of sins that cut off our very relationship with God. "They are filled with every kind of wickedness: maliciousness, greed, ill will, envy, murder, bickering, deceit, craftiness. They are gossips and slanderers, they hate God. . . . One sees in them men without affection, without pity. They know God's just decree that all who do such things deserve death." These are hard words. They cut to the truly destructive power of gossip, not only for those slandered but for the gossiper as well.

Most of us who live in Christian community have had to deal with the tendency to gossip. Oh, it starts innocently enough. Because we truly care for another's well-being, we talk to someone about them. It all comes under the category of "concern." But something usually happens in this discussion. It is as if a little demon is awakened within our soul. We find that speaking about someone else's problems actually makes us *feel good*. In fact, it makes us feel *superior*. Soon we begin speaking about them for our benefit, rather than for theirs! Usually this process is not conscious, nor is it intentional. It is, however, the normal process that happens when we speak about someone else's problems. We call it "concern" to make ourselves feel holy. But gossip is all it really is. And all it usually accomplishes is slander.

St. Francis was well aware of the problem of gossip and slander within the very community of Brothers he formed. He speaks words of equal gravity: "Disaster confronts the Order, unless these slanderers are checked. Quickly the sweetest savor of the many begins to take on a horrible stench, unless the mouths of the stinking are closed." Thomas of Celano continues, "What then is a detractor but the gall of humanity, the leaven of wickedness, the disgrace of the world? What then is a double-tongued man but the scandal of religion, the poison of the cloister, the destroyer of harmony?" St. Bonaventure says, "In Francis's eyes the vice of detraction in particular seemed to be the antithesis of the religious spirit and an enemy of grace. He had a horror of it, like a snake bite or deadly past, and he declared that it was an abomination in God's sight because the detractor feeds on the blood of the souls which he kills with his tongue." Here Francis, too, saw the detractor and the gossip on a par with *and* no better than the murderer.

Francis himself continues in his Rules: "Far from indulging in detraction or disputing in words the friars should do their best to avoid talking, according as God gives them the opportunity. There must be no quarreling among themselves or with others, and they should be content to answer everyone humbly.... They must not give way to anger.... They are to speak evil of none; there must be no complaining, no slander; it is written, 'Whisperers and detractors are people hateful to God' (Rom. 1:29). And let them be moderate, showing all mildness to all men without a word of criticism or condemnation."

St. Clare, too, speaks especially of spreading gossip outside the monastery. "They may not dare to repeat the rumors of the world inside the monastery. And they are strictly bound not to repeat outside the monastery anything that was said or done within which could cause scandal."

Most leaders of Christian communities have had to deal with the tragedy of some person spreading rumors of half-truths outside the immediate community. It can be a nightmare, sometimes destroying whole communities. But in time the rumors die down and the spiritual fruit of the community remains self-evident. As Sirach says of slander and gossip, "Dire is the death it inflicts . . . yet it will not take hold among the just nor scorch them in its flame."

In most communities, the veneer of a false humility wears thin pretty quickly. If anyone comes with an affected piety regarding silence, speaking seldom or always in a quiet tone, it usually lasts about a week or so. After that reality sets in, and the person begins speaking according to what is really in his heart. Often those who seem to have the most "contemplative" manner are the ones who cover up the most lust and anger within.

So a certain amount of human freedom is good in a Christian community. We must have the freedom really to be ourselves, or else our community is living in a lie. Contemplatives do not talk any differently from anyone else. Nor do they walk or sit in a special way. Yes, they should be disciplined, but this discipline is designed to make them more fully human. Contemplatives are not spiritual robots.

In this attempt to be "human" and "approachable," many Christians are forgetting their genuine call to holiness. This is especially true in the area of speech. In an attempt to be human many of us have reverted to coarse language and an occasional dirty joke. The sad thing is that it does not stop there. The more we talk the more we think, and the more we think the more we talk. Soon our words are no different than the words of the world.

Likewise, our words lead us on to action. Soon we are again indulging in the very things Jesus once freed us from. We have given free rein to our tongues, and our tongues have led us back into spiritual and physical bondage.

St. Paul says, "Never let evil talk pass your lips, say only the good things men need to hear, things that will really help them.... As for lewd conduct or promiscuousness or lust of any sort, let them not even be mentioned among you; your holiness forbids this. Nor should there be any obscene, silly, or suggestive talk; all that is out of place." Sirach supports this: "Let not your mouth become used to coarse talk, for in it lies sinful matter.... A man who has the habit of abusive language will never mature in character as long as he lives."

St. Francis alludes to this same thing when he says, "Blessed that religious who finds all his joy and happiness in the words and deeds of our Lord and uses them to make people love God gladly. Woe to that religious who amuses himself with silly gossip, trying to make people laugh."

This is all fine and good, you say. But how do I stop? The habit of an uncontrolled tongue is, without a doubt, one of the most difficult habits to overcome. The problem is only compounded when you live in a community where this fire has burned through the whole house. Besides this, won't my Brothers and Sisters think me snobbish or spiritually proud if I suddenly shy away from the usual jokes and exclamative remarks? There is no question about it. The habit of an uncontrolled tongue is difficult and nearly impossible to break. This is true especially when a whole community is enslaved to the fire of this sin.

Giving Thanks

St. Paul gives us an answer that is so simple it almost sounds absurd. He says, "All that is out of place. Instead, give thanks." That's all there is to it? That's right. Paul's bit of advice—give thanks—is enough to extinguish almost totally the sinful fire of the tongue.

The Fire of the Tongue

Giving thanks is very similar to the antidote for anger and resentment, only it is intentionally spoken. It is not just in our thoughts, but is verbal. This means every time a conversation leans toward gossip and slander, you would be wise to give thanks to God for the person being slandered. Say something really good about them! I do not mean that you should be insensitive to a valid concern, but I do mean always respond with a positive comment about the person in question. At best, respond only with a silence that needs not repeat the tale.

As Sirach says, "He who repeats an evil report has no sense. Never repeat gossip. . . . Let anything you hear die within you; be assured it will not make you burst." I wish we could learn that we need not repeat everything we hear about someone else. He continues, "Admonish your friend—he may not have done it; and if he did, that he may not do it again. Admonish your neighbor—he may not have said it; and if he did, that he may not say it again. Admonish your friend—often it may be slander, every story you must not believe." As he says in another place, "Before investigating, find no fault; examine first, then criticize." We should always respond positively to any negativity we hear. Only then will we, or the person who comes to us, be able to discern the truth that will set all of us free.

This positive response will free your own spirit from the shackles of negativity so that you will be able to see more clearly into the real problem at hand. It may not be the person being spoken of at all. It may be the person doing the speaking.

Likewise, the continual practice of giving thanks will free you and others from the habit of coarse jesting and foul language. When you get into the habit of thanking God for all things, you will find that you just begin to feel better. You will feel fresh and clean inside. It is like being "born again." The more you give thanks, the more you will find that you just don't want to speak in any other way.

By speaking thanks, our minds have to be transformed, for in order to formulate words we must first conceptualize thoughts.

The Fire of God

The more our thoughts are transformed, the more our feelings are lifted to the positive. The more our thoughts are lifted, the easier it is to give thanks. Soon a whole upward spiraling process of thanksgiving and joy totally frees us of the negativity of gossip, slander, and foul language.

It is the speaking forth of thanks that transforms not only our minds but our actions. Sirach says, "A word is the source of every deed; a thought of every act. The root of all conduct is the mind; four branches it shoots forth: Good and evil, death and life, their absolute mistress is the tongue." When we change our words we must change our thoughts, and when we change our thoughts our actions will more easily change. Thus, it is the speaking forth of thanks and praise that can change the downward spiral of our present life of negativity, gossip, and sin, and turn it upward to spiral into God's highest heaven.

By its nature this upward spiral affects all those around you. It is like the winds of a heavenly tornado, only instead of destruction, this tornado transports all within its reach to heaven.

If we begin to speak only positive responses and thanksgivings during our community gatherings and socials, we will make it very difficult for anyone to speak sinfully about anyone or anything. It is not something uncomfortable. It is healthy and freeing. Deep down inside, people genuinely like others who are innocent and who speak without guile. They feel comfortable around those who say only good things about others, for they know only good things will be said about them. As scripture says, "A kind mouth multiplies friends, and gracious lips prompt friendly greetings."

The fire of God that touches the lips of His prophets is stronger than the fire of sin that blisters the lips of the tale-bearer and the coarse jester. If we have the courage to light the fire of God's word in our communities, the sinful fire of the tongue will be extinguished.

But what do we do when none of this seems to work? We sincerely try to clean up our speech and say only good things about other people, but somehow things always go from bad to worse.

Somehow the influence of our associates and friends always seems stronger than our desire to speak only of God. Worse yet, sometimes we are the very ones who get the conversation going in the negative direction! No doubt about it, sometimes we are the ones who are caught in the downward rather than the upward-flowing spiral. No matter how hard we try, we just can't seem to break free.

This is where I, again, recommend prayer in tongues. I know I have already spoken of this several times in this book, but the analogy seems so clear in this case. The only way to break totally free of the destructive fire of the tongue is to replace it with the "tongues of fire" that bring both praise and thanksgiving into our lives with boldness and with power! When the mind is so clouded by negativity that words of thanksgiving which proceed from the mind only lead to stammering and stuttering, then it is time to bypass the mind completely. By praying in the Spirit, the deepest spirit of a human being can pray. It is this spirit that calls out to be set free from the prison of negativity imposed upon it by the slander and coarseness of the external world. By praying in the Spirit the mind is eventually cleansed. When the mind is cleared, then the spoken words of thanksgiving can come more easily. This is exactly the same process used with the fire of lust and the fire of anger, and it works here just as well. Try it if you find it impossible to break free of the destructive fire of your tongue. Replace it with the "tongue of fire" that originates with the very fire of God!

The Discipline of Silence

There is also a healthy asceticism that will further help you control your tongue. It is called, quite simply, "silence." Silence is not a negative concept. It is positive. It is by embracing the discipline of silence that we come to speak the word of God effectively. We must enter into silence if we are to shut out the noises and thoughts of this world. When both our tongue and our mind are still, then we ourselves can clearly hear God's word. Only after hearing God's word will we know what to speak. Then we can replace our foolish words with the very word of God. Silence does not just stop speech, it prunes it!

The scriptures are full of admonitions to a healthy silence, not to the exclusion of speech, but toward its edification. St. James says, "Let every man be quick to hear, slow to speak, slow to anger." Sirach says also, "Be swift to hear, but slow to answer. . . . If you have knowledge, answer your neighbor; if not, put your hand over your mouth." Proverbs says, "In the multitude of words there lacks not sin."

On the positive side Sirach says, "Refrain not from speaking at the proper time, and hide not away your wisdom; for it is through speech that wisdom becomes known," but it still cautions us to be prepared when we speak: "He who studies the law masters it, but the hypocrite finds it a trap. . . . The thoughtful man will not neglect direction. . . . Do nothing without counsel. . . . Prepare your words and you will be listened to; draw upon your training and then give your answer." This balance between silence and speech is again brought out by Sirach: "When invited by a man of influence, keep your distance; then he will urge you all the more. Be not bold with him lest you be rebuffed, but keep not too far away lest you be forgotten. Engage not freely in discussion with him . . . for by prolonged talk he will test you, and through smiling he will probe you."

Again, "An admonition can be inopportune, and a man may be wise to hold his peace. . . . One man is silent and is thought wise, another is talkative and is disliked. One man is silent because he has nothing to say; another is silent, biding his time. A wise man is silent till the right time comes, but a boasting fool ignores the proper time. He who talks too much is detested; he who pretends to authority is hated."

It is against this backdrop that we must place the teachings of Jesus concerning the use of the tongue. Jesus was a devout Jew and no doubt studied the wisdom literature of His faith. His words about words are understandably short and concise. Beyond the gospel teachings we have already considered, He says, "You have heard the commandment imposed on your forefathers. 'Do not take a false oath; rather, make good to the Lord all your pledges.' What I tell you is: do not swear at all.... Say, 'Yes' when you mean 'Yes' and 'No' when you mean 'No.' Anything beyond that comes from the evil one." It is wise to review constantly His words that say, "On judgment day people will be held accountable for every unguarded word they speak." There is no doubt about it; Jesus' words on words are fully consistent with the teaching of the wisdom literature of the Old Testament. He supports a deliberate and concise speech that is, undoubtedly, pruned down for spiritual fruitfulness by the discipline of silence.

St. Francis follows along squarely within this gospel tradition. As we have seen, he says in his first written Rule, "Far from indulging in detraction or disputing in words, the friars should do their best to avoid talking as God gives them the opportunity." In his so-called *Rule For Hermits* he cautions, "They must be careful to keep silence and say their Office" [common liturgical prayer]. This silence is not complete, however, even in the hermitage. He allows for a rhythm between times of silence and speech. This should lead the friars to a genuine reverence for words. It is this reverence that led Francis to encourage the preachers of the Order, saying, "Their words should be examined and chaste. They should aim only at the advantage and spiritual good of their listeners, telling them briefly about vice and virtue, punishment and glory, because our Lord himself kept his words short on earth."

St. Bonaventure continues in the Franciscan tradition when he writes *On the Perfection of Life* to the Franciscan Sisters: "The virtue of silence is of great help to the religious striving for perfection; for as, 'where words are many, sin is not wanting' (Prov. 10:19), so where words are few and short, sin is kept away." He appeals to the tradition of the desert fathers when he says, "To become accustomed to silence, you should follow the example of

89

Abbot Agathon, of whom we read in the *Lives of the Fathers* that he kept a pebble in his mouth for three years, until he had learned to be silent. You too should tie a pebble to your tongue, fix it to your palate, and 'put your hand over your mouth' (Judg. 18:19), so as to learn how to be silent." He then comes back from this analogy to more practical advice, "Speak seldom, with economy and brevity; speak with reverence and modesty. . . . Sew your lips shut with the thread of discipline, let your words be brief, rare, to the point, as well as meek and humble. . . . Speak seldom and sparely. . . . Never fall into idle speech. . . . As the gloss (of Matt. 12:36) explains, 'a word is idle when said without need, and heard without gain.' As a wise man says, 'I have sometimes regretted having spoken, but never, having held my tongue.'"

For me this discipline of silence must happen both on a private and on a communal level. True, it is good to spend time in solitude in order for it to become a further discipline for silence. When you are alone there is really nobody to talk to but God. After saying very little we find ourselves more willing to listen than to talk. Let's face it, God's words carry more weight than our own. Being in God's presence brings us to a silence where it becomes easy to listen. It is by listening that we hear His word, and by hearing His word that we learn again how to speak. As St. Bonaventure says, "Nothing better helps a religious to remain silent than flight from the company of others and the pursuit of a life of solitude."

But sometimes the silence of solitude does apparently little to control the idle and worldly talk of a community. True, the individuals of the community might spend long hours in solitary prayer, meditation, and study. But as soon as the community gathers for social activities everyone can hardly wait to resume with the latest news of the community hotline, or with a veritable flood of idle curiosities and senseless jokes. This is common and indicates that, despite long hours of solitude, true silence of heart and mind has never really been embraced or achieved.

For this reason I strongly recommend times and places for communal silence as well as the private silent times experienced in solitude. It is a real exercise in holding one's tongue to sit around a common table and eat part of a meal in silence. Or to do some manual work with others in silence. Or simply to walk in the woods or around a chapel in silence. All of this teaches us how to relate to one another without words. It teaches us how to communicate in the Spirit without utterances. It opens up another level of communal existence that is usually clouded and hindered by a constant cacophony of spoken words.

When we break through to this new level of spiritual communication as a community, we find it transforms our spoken exchanges as well. Suddenly the community simply does not want to destroy its spiritual tranquility by too many senseless words. Instead of the command of silence being an imposed law, it becomes something we all yearn for and revere in the Spirit. It becomes not only a discipline for appointed times and places, but a whole way of life we willfully choose. Instead of ministering the death of the law, it ministers spirit and life.

All of this is like a light that spreads from the new fire of the dawning sun. Its rays shine forth to chase the darkness away from the earth. What once was blanketed and entrapped in the powers of the night suddenly is freed by the bursting forth of a literal fire of God's light. All is made new. All is reborn. A new day and a whole new way of life lies ahead!

6
The Fire of Nuclear Holocaust

Having looked at some of the fires that destroy our own soul, perhaps we are now better prepared to understand the nuclear issue. We cannot expect to deal with the potential external fire of a sweeping nuclear holocaust if we cannot deal with the destructive fires that sweep through our own human souls. How can we deal with the big problems outside of us if we haven't yet dealt with their cause that still dwells within us? If there is still a major war within our souls, how can we effectively stop wars in the world? We cannot.

There will always be a struggle with sin in our own souls. Paul says, "I cannot even understand my own actions. I do not do what I want to do but what I hate. . . . If I do what is against my will, it is not I who do it, but sin which dwells in me." John says, "If we say 'We are free of the guilt of sin' we deceive ourselves." We will never be totally free of the struggle with sin. If we wait for this before we act, we will never do anything. We cannot effectively act before God has acted within us, but neither can we wait to act until we are totally perfect or we will never act at all.

Likewise, Jesus never really gives us a promise that we will ever achieve world peace. He says that even at the end of time, "You will hear of wars and rumors of wars. Do not be alarmed. Such things are bound to happen, but that is not yet the end. Nation will rise against nation, and one kingdom against another." Scripture even indicates there will be a time of false peace at the end of time: "Just when people are saying, 'Peace and security,' ruin will fall on them with the suddenness of pains overtaking a woman in labor, and there will be no escape."

Jesus gives us a peace, but it is not a peace of this world. It is an internal peace that passes all understanding. He says, "'Peace' is my farewell to you, my peace is my gift to you; I do not give it to you as the world gives peace. Do not be distressed or fearful."

Jesus takes a very passive view toward the prospect of a particular government bringing peace to this war-torn world. Jesus lived under what His people viewed to be an oppressive unjust government. Many Jewish religious sects advocated strong political involvement, but Jesus was passive at best. "Give to Caesar what is Caesar's, but give to God what is God's." Paul follows this course concerning the militant and oppressive Roman Government when he says, "Let everyone obey the authorities that are over him, for there is no authority except from God . . . the man who opposes authority rebels against the ordinance of God. . . . It is not without purpose that the ruler carries the sword; he is God's servant, to inflict his avenging wrath on the wrongdoer. . . . Pay each one his due: taxes to whom taxes are due; toll to whom toll is due; respect and honor to everyone who deserves them."

Peter follows a similar course in his letter: "Because of the Lord, be obedient to every human institution, whether to the emperor as sovereign or to the governors he commissions for the punishment of criminals and the recognition of the upright. Such obedience is the will of God." Ironically all three—Jesus, Peter, and Paul—died at the hands of these very governments! Yet their obedience and nonresistance did not waver. As Jesus said even to the weak-willed Pontius Pilate, "You would have no power over me whatever unless it were given you from above."

Jesus, Peter, and Paul are simply not political activists. They are not *excessive* liberation theologians. They bring a liberty of the Spirit and a peace that passes all understanding. A peace that perseveres whether externally at war or in peace. A life of peace and justice that persists even through an unjust and brutal death.

This does not mean, of course, that we should not work for external peace. The Psalmist says, "Seek and strive after peace." Jesus says, "Blessed are the peacemakers," granted that this peace is primarily internal, in the soul, and external in the Church and the world. Paul says, "Christ's peace must reign in your hearts, since as members of the one body you have been called to that peace."

But this peace also extends out to the world, as Paul counsels, "If possible, live peaceably with everyone."

We might rightly recognize that Jesus never promised world peace. We might rightly recognize that we will always have poverty and war. As He also says, "The poor you have with you always." But this does not mean that we should stop being charitable or stop working for peace. As Jesus says concerning evil in the world, "Woe to the world because of the things that cause people to sin! Such things must come, but woe to the man through whom they come!" Are we instruments of war or peace? We may never totally establish peace in this age, but we must still dedicate our life to working for it.

If we are not ready to stay and work for peace on this earth, then we will never be ready to go to our heavenly peace. We are ready to go only if we are prepared to stay, and we are able to stay only if we are prepared to go at any given time. We must live on earth as if we were preparing it for the eternal peace of the kingdom of God. Otherwise we are not ready to spend eternity on the "new heavens and new earth where, according to his promise, the justice of God will reside." If we are not willing to work for peace and social justice on earth, we are not yet able to pass on to the place of God's eternal peace and justice.

The concept of nuclear war obviously cannot be found in scripture. The Bible describes a warfare that was "conventional" to the times, limited in its destructive power to person-to-person or soldier-to-soldier ratios. Such was the warfare of swords, arrows, and spears. Most wars of history have been of this type where the destruction caused by one soldier or nation affected only a limited or targeted group of soldiers or people of an enemy nation.

The closest thing to a nuclear holocaust is found in the second epistle of Peter regarding the day of the Lord. "The day of the Lord will come like a thief, and on that day the heavens will vanish with a roar; the elements will be destroyed by fire; and the earth and all its deeds will be made manifest . . . the heavens will be destroyed in flames and the elements will melt in a blaze." There are also the list of environmental woes and plagues described in the Apocalypse that could imaginatively be seen as the aftereffects of a nuclear war.

All these things have been interpreted as the consequence of God's just wrath on a habitually obstinate and sinful people. In a way they serve as biblical reminders that the fire of a nuclear holocaust will come only if we in our sin permit it. There are steps we can take to prevent it. If we do not take them, then its eventuality will come as a kind of just recompense for both our individual and collective sins as a modern people. I do not say these passages of scripture deal directly with the problem of nuclear war. I only say they stand as reminders. This scripture likewise reminds us that total peace will come only in heaven. "What we await are new heavens and a new earth where according to his promise, the justice of God will reside."

Nuclear war is not a clear part of scripture, and its potentially destructive power is hard even to imagine. It will destroy not only military personnel and property but entire populations. It will destroy not only the present but the future through environmental contamination and the mutation of human beings. No one really knows the full effects of a nuclear war, for there has never been an all-out nuclear exchange. But we do know it would, in fact, change the course and complexion of what we call the human race. It would be an atrocity, a horrendous holocaust unequaled in the past history of war.

To really "win" a nuclear war, governments say they need first-strike capabilities. This means not allowing one enemy warhead to detonate within your national boundaries. It means an impenetrable defense. It means having the first jump in offense. First-strike capabilities are truly mind boggling. This means that you have to knock out every missile silo, every submarine, and every nuclear bomber the other side possesses. If even one enemy missile gets through you lose hundreds, thousands, perhaps even millions of lives!

Such destruction is clearly immoral for any reason. What kind of world would be left after such a holocaust? Even if we won, what would we win? What would be left? Are we really willing to destroy millions upon millions of innocent victims in order to save our own country?

More than likely, first-strike success would not be complete. Not only would we destroy millions within enemy boundaries, but millions of our own would also die. It would be mass devastation. This kind of mass destruction cannot be deemed moral by any definition. To win you must be ready to strike first. If you do this you must be the aggressor. This cannot be deemed moral by any Christian definition of a "just war."

Would it not actually be better to disarm unilaterally? Simply to refuse to use nuclear weapons at all is surely the only moral way in the face of such a holocaust. If we play bluff at the bargaining table in the arms race, we must be willing to use those arms. Otherwise our bluff is itself a lie and a self-deceit. If we use the arms at all we become immoral as a nation. The only moral option is to disarm bilaterally, or if we must, unilaterally. Of course bilateral disarmament is the first and more appealing option.

This does not mean we would refuse resistance to a Communist takeover. If the United States unilaterally disarmed, the people of the United States would have to make it emphatically clear to any Communist nation that we would nonviolently resist on every domestic level. Faced with such nonviolent noncooperation, no foreign power could overcome us without killing us all. Then the question would arise: Would we rather use our nuclear weapons and take the world with us, or would we sacrifice our own lives in the name of human life and peace? I could only pray we would take the moral rather than the immoral option.

While recognizing the civil government's right to use the just force of "an eye for an eye" to keep the peace, and the right of a nation to defend itself with conventional arms in the self-defense of the traditional "just war," the Church has unhesitantly condemned the use of nuclear arms and the arms race. In the *Constitution of the Church in the Modern World*, the Catholic Church speaks clearly on the question of nuclear arms: "Acts of war involving these weapons can inflict massive and indiscriminate destruction, thus going far beyond the bounds of legitimate defense. Indeed, if the kind of instruments which can now be found in the armories of the great nations were to be employed to their fullest, an almost total and altogether reciprocal slaughter of each side by the other would follow, not to mention the widespread devastation that would take place in the world and the deadly aftereffects that would be spawned by the use of weapons of this kind. All these considerations compel us to undertake an evaluation of war with an entirely new attitude."

The old laws about war are no longer relevant. It is almost as if God has allowed us to see the ultimate end of war in order to force the whole human race to a decision: If we continue to choose war, we will now destroy ourselves.

As to the legitimacy of "détente," or the deterrence of nuclear war by a mutual build-up of nuclear arms, the Church is again clear. "Many regard this as the most effective way by which peace of a sort can be maintained between nations at the present time. . . . Men should be convinced that the arms race in which an already considerable number of countries are engaged is not a safe way to preserve a steady peace. The causes of war are in danger of being gradually aggravated. . . . The arms race is an utterly treacherous trap for humanity."

A Change of Heart

What, then, are we to do? The Church document continues. "It is our clear duty, therefore, to strain every muscle in working for the time when all war can be completely outlawed by international consent. . . . Everyone must labor to put an end at last to the arms race, and to make a true beginning of disarmament, not unilaterally indeed, but proceeding at an equal pace according to agreement, and backed up by adequate and workable safe-guards."

This means that both Catholic and non-Catholic Christians should mobilize as a transgovernmental body across the earth to move the governments of their respective nations to work for peace. This is done by exercising the right to free speech and the power of the vote in free nations. In nations without this freedom, the Christians must form a powerful, but discrete, underground to promote the social justice that leads to peace. Again I would even advocate a nonviolent noncooperation with clearly immoral governmental powers.

All of this leads us back to where we started: the fire of materialism. Where there is materialism by some, there is poverty for others. And where there is poverty, there is a cause for war, either in the greed of those who have too much and will not share, or in the desperation of those who need at least a little in order to survive. Both extremes cause war. Where there is war, there is the potential of nuclear war. We must fight against rampant materialism and poverty, and if we want to stop rampant materialism and poverty we must first change the human heart. This can fully happen only through sharing the spiritual reality of the gospel of Jesus Christ.

As the Church teaches: "In order to build up peace the causes of discord among men, especially injustice, which ferment wars, must above all be rooted out. Not a few of these causes come from excessive inequalities and from putting off steps needed to remedy them. Other causes of discord, however, have their source in the desire to dominate and in a contempt for persons. And, if we look for deeper causes, we find them in human envy, distrust, pride, and other egotistical passions."

The human heart is a microcosm of the whole world. Any major troubles in our world can be traced back to problems in the human heart. If we want to stamp out the causes of a potential nuclear war in the world, we must first look within and stamp out the causes of war that rage within our human souls. If we want to prevent the fire of a nuclear holocaust, we must first extinguish the fires of selfishness and sin in our own souls. As St. Paul says, "Get rid of all bitterness, all passion and anger, harsh words, slander and malice of every kind. In place of these, be kind to one another, compassionate, and mutually forgiving, just as God has forgiven you in Christ." Until we do this in our own souls, we cannot bring peace to others. And until peace is spread to others of this world, the threat of nuclear war remains.

This means ridding ourselves of the fires of the tongue, anger, and lust. This means extinguishing the fire of materialism. We must distribute our wealth among the poor if we want to solve the root problem of global social injustice and the threat of global extinction through war.

As the Catholic Church teaches, "Do not let men, then, be scandalized because some countries with a majority of citizens who are counted as Christians have an abundance of wealth, whereas others are deprived of the necessities of life and tormented with hunger, disease, and every kind of misery.... Those Christians are to be praised and supported, therefore, who volunteer their services to help other men and nations ... out of the substance of their goods, and not only out of what is superfluous.... Wherever it seems fitting, this activity of Catholics should be carried out in unison with other Christian brothers."

Beyond this the Church encourages participation in organizations committed to peace and social justice. This should occur on the individual and national levels. The Church encourages its own members on the level of God's supernatural laws. It encourages all the world on the level of God's natural laws at work in all creation and in every human soul. These natural laws lead us all to the supernatural.

In this the Church encourages entire nations to take steps toward a just distribution of the world's goods among the peoples of all the earth. This, in turn, helps promote global peace. "The present solidarity of mankind also calls for a revival of greater international cooperation in the economic field.... The development of a nation depends on human and financial aids. The citizens of each country must be prepared by education and professional training.... This requires the aid of foreign specialists who ... will not act as overlords, but as helpers and fellow workers.... Such help should be accorded with generosity and without greed.... If an authentic economic order is to be established on a world-wide basis, an end will have to be put to profiteering, to national ambition, to the appetite for political supremacy, to militaristic calculations, and to the machinations for the purpose of spreading and imposing ideologies."

Again, all of these steps are made possible by the power of the citizen to vote. Where there is not a political option that properly represents the Catholic or non-Catholic Christian perspective, we have the obligation to create one. Jesus and Paul may have been passive toward the oppressive government of Rome precisely because Rome offered no options. We live in a free country. We have the right to have our view represented. If neither the Democrats nor the Republicans express the necessary morality, then it is time to come up with another option!

This necessary morality is embraced by Catholics and non-Catholics alike. We represent a veritable army of people who span every state of our nation, and more importantly, span across every nation on the face of the earth. We are a divine kingdom that spans across human nations. It is time to mobilize. It is time to act for peace and justice. It is time to make the nonviolent force of our morality known. The alternative in this materialistic and war-torn world is death. It is time to make our voice for peace heard!

But more than looking to the problems of a particular political system we must look to the problems that lurk within our own human hearts. If we want to stop the problem of sin in the world, we must first stop sin in our own personal lives. This can be done effectively only by the grace of God through Jesus Christ. No political system will save us, but Jesus will. No peace and social justice commission can help us unless we accept and know His peace and His justification! All external measures for peace and justice will eventually fail without Jesus Christ. This remains the primary proclamation of the Church. This is the core from which all other activities grow, and all Christian political activities must lead back to this spiritual core. The external without the internal is vain. The branches without the Vine will die. Our involvement in the affairs of nations will come to nothing if it does not begin and end in the spiritual reality of the kingdom of heaven. The gospel of Jesus Christ and His kingdom, which transcends all earthly nations, remains the primary message and proclamation of the Church.

From this perspective the most powerful tool we Christians have is the power of prayer. Jesus said that the most powerful thing we can do in the face of the enemy is to love that enemy and pray for him: "Love your enemies, pray for your persecutors." Paul encourages us not only to submit peacefully to government leaders, but to pray for them: "I urge that petitions, prayers, intercessions, and thanksgiving be offered for all men, especially for kings and those in authority that we may be able to lead undisturbed and tranquil lives in perfect piety and dignity."

Here we are enjoined in scripture to pray specifically for religious liberty, basic human rights, and peace. We need to pray against the atheism and religious suppression of the Communists. We need to pray against the materialism of the Capitalists. And we need to pray ardently that these two major forces of this world find a way for nuclear disarmament and eventual peace.

The conclusion of Paul's encouragement for Christians to pray for government leaders emphasizes that all people would come to a saving knowledge of Jesus Christ. "Prayer of this kind is good, and God our savior is pleased with it, for he wants all men to be saved and come to know the truth. And the truth is this: God is one. One also is the mediator between God and men, the man Jesus Christ, who gave himself as a ransom for all."

Jesus is the final peace for this world. He is our justice. He makes us all equal before God. He is the truth that sets us free. He is our lasting liberty. He is the King of Kings and the Prince of Peace. He alone is able to set up a lasting kingdom in which dwell justice and peace. All other lasting attempts must begin and end in Him.

To conclude, I would like to refer to the example of St. Francis. Francis was clearly committed to the preaching of the gospel of Jesus Christ. He traveled across national boundaries to propagate His spiritual kingdom which transcends all earthly kingdoms. Yet he did not hesitate to speak out to governmental leaders in order to establish justice and peace. He established peace between Church and civil leaders in Assisi. He also spoke out boldly against the militarism and materialism of entire towns. Likewise, he traveled to the Holy Land to try and establish peace between the Islamic Sultan and the Christian crusaders. In this he rebuked both, but in a way that positively encouraged peace. He wrote an entire letter of admonition to the rulers of all the people, encouraging religious freedom, social justice, and lasting peace. It would be incorrect to imagine St. Francis of Assisi as a social activist or a liberation freedom fighter, but he was concerned about the peace and social justice established and maintained by and between the civil governments of his own time. In all this, the preaching of the kingdom of Jesus remained primary. But for Francis this kingdom went out from the Church to all of the created world that has been reconciled back to God through Jesus Christ.

7
The Fire of Illumination

Moving from the fires of sin through the fires of purgation, we now consider the divine fire of illumination. This fire is a blazing light that begins to illuminate a person's whole soul. It comes when we begin to meditate on the divine mysteries and find our whole soul enrapt in a fire of ecstatic love. Once the mind and soul have been substantially cleansed of the stain of sin, they begin to reflect the very brightness of the fire of God. Thus, the human soul becomes a mirror of Christ Jesus, who was the perfect mirror of the flame of His heavenly Father.

St. Bonaventure speaks of this passing from the way of purgation to the way of illumination by and through union with God. Bonaventure also uses this image of the human soul becoming a mirror of the divine mind of God in his work, *The Journey of the Mind to God*. He speaks of looking into the creation and into the scripture as a sure way of being illuminated by the fire of God's light. He does say, however, "I am supposing that the mirror offered by the outside world is of little or no value, useless, if the mirror of the mind is not clear and polished. Therefore . . . train yourself by heeding the sharp goad of conscience before you lift up your eyes to the beams of wisdom reflected in the mirrors . . . lest you fall into a deep pit of darkness for having gazed upon such light."

Creation

For the Franciscan school of mysticism the first place the fire-purged soul looks for illumination is to the created world. Bonaventure continues: "In our present condition, the created universe itself is a ladder leading us toward God. . . . Let us place the first of the ascending rungs at the bottom, by setting before ourselves the whole material world as a mirror through which we can step up to God, the supreme Craftsman."

When the scales of sin have fallen from our eyes, all of the world begins to sparkle. When the fire of our sin has ceased sending obscuring smoke and haze into our spiritual eyes, then all of the created world seems to be on fire with God's love. It becomes a veritable "burning bush" that is all afire but not consumed. Its light is everywhere, but it is a fire that does not destroy. It is a fire that illumines the darkness of night and saves. Thomas à Kempis says in his *Imitation of Christ*, "If your heart were right, then every created thing would be a mirror to life and a book of holy doctrine, for no creature is so small and mean that it cannot display God's goodness."

As Bonaventure concludes, "Whoever is not enlightened by such brilliance of things created must be blind; whoever is not awakened by their mighty voice must be deaf; whoever fails to praise God for all his works must be dumb (mute); whoever fails to discover the First Principle through all these signs must be a fool. Open your eyes, then, alert your spiritual ears, unseal your lips, and 'apply your heart' (Prov. 22:17), so that in all your creatures you may see, hear, praise, love, and serve, glorify and honor your God, lest the whole world rise against you."

We cannot climb this natural ladder or see this divine illumination without God's grace and gift of the Spirit. As Bonaventure also says, "Yet we cannot rise above ourselves unless a superior power lifts us up. No matter how well we plan our spiritual progress, nothing comes of it unless a divine assistance intervenes.

Scripture

This divine assistance leads us from the natural world to the greatest of all tools to aid in the soul's illumination—the scriptures. For the Franciscan school it is the scriptures that remain the greatest revelation of the fire of God for His Church. Francis based his life on a literal imitation of Christ. This life of Jesus Christ is best perceived in the gospels, which form the pivotal point of the New Testament scripture.

Bonaventure says in his work *The Breviloquium* that creation and the scriptures work together to form a kind of "Jacob's ladder" that leads us to God. In this analogy, philosophy, which is the study of the created universe, forms the first rung and has its foot resting firmly on the earth. The study of scripture, or theology, is the top of the ladder that pierces through to the illuminating light of heaven itself. As Bonaventure says of this scripture study we call theology, "It uses philosophical knowledge as its servant, borrowing from the natural order what it needs to make a mirror for the representation of things divine; erecting, as it were, a ladder, whose foot rests on the earth but whose top reaches heaven."

Of the reading of scripture Bonaventure says emphatically, "No one can penetrate its meaning unless he has first had infused into him faith in Jesus Christ as the lamp, the door, and also the foundation of the entire scriptures." As he says again in *The Journey of the Mind to God*, "Let us not believe that it is enough to read without unction, to speculate without devotion, to investigate without wonder, to observe without joy, to act without godly zeal, to know without love, to understand without humility, to strive without divine grace, or to reflect as a mirror without divinely inspired wisdom."

That is the way St. Francis read the scriptures. Bonaventure says of him, "St. Francis had never studied the Sacred Scriptures, but unwearied application to prayer and the continual practice of virtue had purified his spiritual vision, so that his keen intellect was bathed in the radiance of eternal light and penetrated its depths. Free from every stain, his genius pierced to the heart of its mysteries and by effective love he entered where theologians and their science stand outside. Once he had read something in the sacred books and understood its meaning, he impressed it indelibly on his memory; anything he had once grasped carefully, he meditated upon continuously." This is why the theologians of his era said of him: "His theology soars aloft on the wings of purity and contemplation, like an eagle in full flight, while our learning crawls along on the ground."

Visualization

In the use of scripture and the created world the healthy use of our human faculty of imagination helps us to touch the very mind of God. This means allowing the imagination to break through beyond the realm of cold, static ideas into a whole new spiritual world that is fully alive in Christ.

St. Bonaventure speaks of this process in his meditations on the life of Christ. More than any other school of Christian spirituality of that era, the Franciscan school emphasized a positive and healthy use of the imagination in visualizing the earthly life of Jesus Christ to draw us spiritually closer to His heavenly glory where He sits at the right hand of the Father.

As St. Bonaventure says, "Imagination assists understanding." In developing his meditation *The Tree of Life*, the Saint encourages the reader actually to "Picture in your imagination a tree." He then goes on to correlate various parts of the tree to the various aspects of both the earthly and heavenly life of Christ. As he says, we must meditate on Christ "with vivid representation, penetrating intelligence, and loving will." According to Bonaventure, this will help stir up the soul to love. Meditation of this sort will help us to "enkindle an affection" for Jesus Christ.

Do you use your mind in a creative way during prayer, or do you try to stifle your imagination because you have read somewhere that a "real contemplative" prays without the use of mental images or words? True, at certain stages of contemplation we will pass over into this imageless prayer; but especially at the beginning of prayer, we should direct our thoughts through healthy meditation, which involves a healthy use of the imagination.

Distracting Thoughts

This practice also helps us with distracting thoughts during times of prayer. How many of us have not battled against an assault of distracting thoughts when we finally set aside quality time for meditation or prayer? It is hard enough just to find the time. When we finally find the time, it's quality is destroyed by those unwelcome and uncontrollable "intruders." Seemingly from nowhere our mind is filled with wild and crazy thoughts. People and places from our past. Sins we thought we have been in control of for years. Sins we never even dreamed of committing. All these things, and more, assail us once we have the courage to get serious about setting aside intentional settings and times for prayer.

As I pointed out in my book, *The Lover and the Beloved*, St. Francis also had to deal with such thoughts. Even the holiest of the desert fathers and the fathers of the Church comment on the endless parade of distracting ideas that intruded upon their thoughts during times of prayer. Francis found himself thinking about insignificant hobbies. St. Augustine repeatedly saw sensuous dancing girls. We, too, have our own memories and activities of the present and future to distract us from an undistracted encounter with God.

Usually it is not enough simply to say, "replace distracting thoughts with thoughts about God." Try as I might, this quickly degenerates into an activity of brute force rather than an activity of love. I grit my teeth, clench my fist and try to drive the thoughts away by an iron-like control of my mind. But most of the time I lose! This whole process becomes a "law" for me that, try as I might to obey, I am unable to keep. The harder I try the more I fail. The more I fail, the more guilt-ridden I become. The more guilty I become, the more I tend to cross over that fine line between depression and despair. This despair, I know, will lead me to spiritual death.

Sometimes it helps me actually to use the distractions to lead me to God. It might be a temptation to lust or sexual immorality. If I use this temptation to remind me of the ultimate fulfillment of my spiritual sexuality in Christ, the temptation loses its destructive power. My basic sexuality actually becomes a point of meditation to lead me to Jesus, who is the Bridegroom of my soul.

Almost any thought can be redirected and become an opportunity for prayer. Whatever faculty of the human person that is aroused, be it for holy or unholy reasons, is a reflection of the nature of God. The temptation might be unholy, but the human person remains a reflection of the image of God. Most sin is but a perversion of the truth. Immorality is but a perversion of morality. The devil is not that creative! According to the desert fathers, the devil cannot create anything. He can only pervert and mimic. He only perverts the good and wholesome things that God created. Thus, even our temptations to sin can be redirected to lead us to a meditation on the nature of God.

If I am tempted to lie, for example, it can lead me to meditate on the truth of God. If I am tempted to abuse power, it can lead me to meditate on God's omnipotence. If I am tempted to anger, it can lead me to meditate on God's mildness and patience, and on God's eventual show of *just* wrath. If I am tempted to speak angry words, this can lead me to meditate on Jesus, the ultimate Word of love spoken by the Father in the Holy Spirit.

Of course, even this process can prove to be futile. It can degenerate into a mere mental gymnastic that proves to be almost useless in leading us into spiritual union with God. Furthermore, for the beginner it can become a dangerous game of playing with fire. We think, for instance, that we can redirect our thought of sin to a meditation on the righteous nature of God, but all we are finally able to do is to give in to the temptation to sin like a candle melting into formless wax before a hot flame.

As we have seen, it is often the prayer of tongues that releases our spirit to pray in the Spirit of God. It is the active and intentional stirring up of the flame of the Spirit that can renew our minds. It is then the work of God's grace, and not human works, that purifies the mind and prepares it for creative meditation. It is this grace-filled meditation that opens the mind for yet more grace so that, grace building upon grace, our mind and our spirit can mount up the ladder of God into the very heights of heaven!

Eventually, however, this all comes back to a healthy use of visualization in meditation. Rather than prematurely seeing all images and conceptualizations as barriers to contemplative prayer, we should see them as aids ushering us into contemplative prayer. They are the rungs of the ladder to heaven. Which way we go on this ladder, up or down, descending or ascending, is up to us.

8
Moses: The Fire of Sinai

The scriptures are filled with references to God as a fire that will illuminate our very soul. Remember how Moses saw an angel of the Lord in the burning bush on Mt. Horeb: "He came to Horeb, the mountain of God. There an angel of the Lord appeared to him in a fire flaming out of a bush. As he looked on, he was surprised to see that the bush, though on fire, was not consumed. So Moses decided, 'I must go over to look at this remarkable sight, and see why the bush is not burned.'" Here we see the image of God as a fire at the very beginning of Moses' call from God. This fire is not a fire of destruction. It is a fire of salvation for a people in bondage. It is a fire that sets prisoners and slaves free! The fire on Mt. Horeb does not destroy even a thing as frail as a bush. Its flames burst up from the tiny little bush, yet the bush is not consumed!

The greatest mystical revelation of God in all the Old Testament is connected to this image of fire. From the burning bush God will call out and speak to Moses. He will warn Moses of His awesome holiness: "Come no nearer! Remove the sandals from your feet, for the place where you stand is holy ground." Moses will first be afraid: "Moses hid his face, for he was afraid to look at God." But then God will make the greatest revelation of His divine name and being. God reveals Himself as the great I AM! "I am who am. This is what you shall tell the Israelites: I AM sent me to you."

In scripture this I AM reveals God as a pure being of totally underived existence. It is to this revelation of God that Jesus identifies His own divine origins when He said to the Jews, "I solemnly declare it: before Abraham came to be, I AM."

The awesome reality of this revelation of God is overwhelming to the human soul, and once perceived (I say perceived because it is too great to be totally understood), will burn within its depths with a knowing that passes all knowledge. It is a knowledge that burns like a fire deep within the human soul, yet does not destroy.

The soul, like the frail little bush on Mt. Horeb, will burn with this fire of the call and revelation of God, yet will not be consumed. It will be saved!

We know that this figure of fire is seen throughout the deliverance of Israel from the slavery of Egypt. As they left their land of bondage they ventured forth in faith into the complete unknown of the desert. Without God's direction they would surely have been lost. Yet, "The Lord preceded them, in the daytime by means of a column of cloud to show them the way, and at night by means of a column of fire to give them light. Thus they could travel both day and night. Neither the column of cloud by day nor the column of fire by night ever left its place in front of the people."

The fire of God is a guiding light for us. We must venture forth in faith into the unknown if we are to come out of our personal slavery to materialism and sin. We must break away from cultures of injustice and oppression, even if it means venturing forth into the darkness and the unknown. Sometimes this will seem like we are venturing forth from the material security and abundance of Egypt into the perils of the desert. Sometimes it means being unafraid of moving forward in the dark. In Egypt we might be enslaved, but at least we were secure! We knew we were slaves, but at least we could see what lay ahead of us. We must be willing to risk the desert if we are ever to be free of our personal enslavement to materialism and sin. We must be willing to venture forth from injustice and oppression into the darkness and the unknown if we are to follow the fire of God's freedom and light. If we are willing to risk, the fire of God will always go before us to be our light. He will never abandon or forsake us.

As the Israelites went forth into the desert they did, in fact, begin to hunger. They began to lament and complain to Moses. "Would that we had died at the Lord's hand in the land of Egypt, as we sat by the fleshpots and ate our fill of bread! But you had to lead us into this desert to make the whole community die of famine!"

Here, again, God speaks salvation from the theophany of the pillar of smoke and fire: "Moses said to Aaron, 'Tell the whole

Israelite community: Present yourselves before the Lord, for he has heard your grumbling.' When Aaron announced this to the whole Israelite community, they turned toward the desert, and lo, the glory of the Lord appeared in the cloud! The Lord spoke to Moses and said, 'I have heard the grumbling of the Israelites. Tell them: In the evening twilight you shall eat flesh, and in the morning you shall have your fill of bread, so that you may know that I, the Lord, am your God.'"

God meets the needs of a people willing to risk. The Israelites had first to turn toward the emptiness of the desert before they could see the pillar of God's glory! They had to look squarely into the place of their hunger before they could be fed. They had to look squarely into the face of their own sin before they could really be free of the slavery of Egypt in the promised land. They had to realize that the real Egypt was within them all! They had to gaze into this place of thirst and death before they could be given the water of life. Only after facing squarely the source of their hunger could they hear the word of the Lord that promised the bread from heaven to a people who were hungering in the desert.

For us of the New Covenant, Jesus is this Bread from heaven. As Jesus says, "I myself am the Bread of Life. No one who comes to me shall ever be hungry." God speaks salvation to us from fire, and He sends us deliverance and fulfillment in Jesus.

St. Bonaventure tells how Francis of Assisi "burned with love for the Sacrament of our Lord's Body with all his heart, and was lost in wonder at the thought of such condescending love, such loving condescension. He received Holy Communion often and so devoutly that he roused others to devotion too. The presence of the Immaculate Lamb used to take him out of himself, so that he was often lost in ecstasy." Bonaventure was speaking about a mystical fire that enveloped Francis's entire soul with the whole soul of Christ. If Francis burned with love for the Eucharist, it was only because he burned with love for Christ Himself. In the Eucharist he saw the very condescension of Christ, and was moved to burning love.

115

Of this continuing condescension Francis says, "Every day he humbles himself just as he did when he came from his heavenly throne into the Virgin's womb; every day he comes to us and lets us see his abjection, when he descends from the bosom of the Father into the hands of the priest at the altar. He shows himself to us in this sacred bread just as he once appeared to his apostles in real flesh. With their own eyes they saw only flesh, but they believed that he was God, because they contemplated him with the eyes of the spirit. We, too, with our own eyes, see only bread and wine, but we must see further and firmly believe that this is his most holy Body and Blood, living and true."

For Francis his love for the Eucharist was intimately connected to his love for the incarnation of God through Jesus Christ. To believe in one led ultimately to the belief in the other. This belief was centered on the assurance that God loves us so much that He comes into the world He created to save it. He took on flesh to save all flesh. This belief was not mere speculation for Francis. It was a mystical fire that burned within his whole soul, and this fire did not destroy, it saved.

The Old Testament story about the manna from heaven does bring out something else. It brings out the legitimacy of making our needs known to God. Jesus says, "Ask and you will receive." Paul says, "At every opportunity pray in the Spirit, using prayers and petitions of every sort." Our Father knows we have needs, and He wants us to trust Him enough to feel free to ask anything of Him. God hears the cries of the poor, and He answers them!

Yet we must be careful about grumbling too often before God. We know that this grumbling angered God and burdened Moses so much that he actually wished he would die. "When Moses heard the people, family after family, crying at the entrance of their tents, so that the Lord became very angry, he was grieved." This kind of grumbling is not faith. It is selfish and immature. This kind of poverty is not the kind Jesus calls "blessed." It is just as ugly and faithless as the self-serving materialism of the rich. It was this continual grumbling that eventually led to the rebellion and faithlessness of the Israelites. It was this that lengthened their sojourn in the desert from a matter of days to the punishment of forty years!

As Hebrews says, "Who were those who revolted when they heard God's voice? Was it not all whom Moses had led out of Egypt? With whom was God angry for forty years? Was it not those who had sinned, whose corpses fell in the desert? To whom but to the disobedient did he swear that they would not enter into his rest? We see, moreover, that it was their unbelief that kept them from entering." This grumbling led from unbelief to actual revolt against God. Instead of leading to salvation it led to death.

God also came as a fire when establishing the covenant at Mt. Sinai. Next to God revealing Himself as the great I AM, this is undoubtedly the next most important event in the entire Old Testament. It was at Sinai that God would deliver His words to the people through Moses. He says, "Therefore, if you hearken to my voice and keep my covenant, you shall be my special possession, dearer to me than all other people, though all the earth is mine. You shall be to me a kingdom of priests, a holy nation." It is significant that during both revelations God came to His chosen people in the theophany of fire!

Before the giving of the Covenant God said, "I am coming to you in a dense cloud, so that when the people hear me speaking with you, they may always have faith in you also." Notice this is not a theophany merited by faith. It is to establish faith among a faithless people!

So many times God works wonders in our lives, but we take the credit. We assume that just because God is working a wonder through our lives that our lives are holy. This is not always the case. Jesus says that on the last day many will say, "'Lord, Lord, have we not prophesied in your name? Have we not exorcised demons by its power? Did we not do many miracles in your name as well?' Then I will declare to them solemnly, 'I never knew you. Out of my sight, you evildoers!'" It is not enough simply to have God work through us. We must give ourselves to God. Here God works miracles to establish faith, not because we have merited miracles by faith. The people were faithless, but God was faithful. The people were weak, but God was strong. The miracle was worked among the faithless to bring a people unto faith.

The account continues: "On the morning of the third day there were peaks of thunder and lightning, and a heavy cloud over the mountain, and a very loud trumpet blast, so that all the people in the camp trembled. . . . Mt. Sinai was all wrapped in smoke, for the Lord came down upon it in fire. The smoke rose from it as though from a furnace, and the whole mountain trembled violently. The trumpet blast grew louder and louder, while Moses was speaking and God answering him with thunder. When the Lord came down to the top of Mt. Sinai, he summoned Moses to the top of the mountain, and Moses went up to him."

This account sounds strikingly similar to the description of God speaking through the natural phenomenon of a fiery volcano! Whether or not this is the case is not important. What is important is that this fire of God was an awesome experience. The invisible God was manifesting Himself to His people through a powerful, earthshaking fire atop a huge mountain! The point is clear: God is powerful and almighty, yet He chooses to deal mercifully with His weak and lowly people.

This encounter with the Almighty is not to be taken lightly. The people must prepare for the coming of God. "Go to the people and have them sanctify themselves today and tomorrow. Make them wash their garments and be ready for the third day; for on the third day the Lord will come down on Mt. Sinai before the eyes of all the people." This prefigures the coming of God in the New Covenant through the rising of Jesus from the dead on the third day.

Likewise, not just anyone can go up the mountain. The mountain is holy, and only those expressly chosen by God may ascend its slopes into the cloud of fire. "Set limits for the people all around the mountain, and tell them: Take care not to go up the mountain, or even to touch its base. If anyone touches the mountain, he must be put to death."

Do we really prepare for the coming of the Lord in our life? Jesus encourages us in the parable of the ten virgins: "Keep your eyes open, for you know not the day or the hour of this coming." The five foolish virgins were not prepared, while the five wise virgins were. Are we prepared?

In the parable of the wedding banquet Jesus rebukes those who come improperly dressed, even though they had been invited. To those not properly dressed for the solemn occasion He says, "Bind him hand and foot and throw him out into the night to wail and grind his teeth." He concludes: "The invited are many, the elect are few."

Do we reverence the solemnity of God as we approach Him? Do we really value the merciful invitation given to us by the Bridegroom? As the second epistle of Peter says, "Be solicitous to make your call and election permanent." We must not take the mercy of God for granted!

The wording of the Exodus account would suggest that the very fire of God would slay those who approach the mountain irreverently. The fire spoke of deliverance from the burning bush. The Lord spoke from the fire when He revealed Himself as I AM. The fire went before Israel to deliver them from bondage and to be their light in the darkness. Yet here this same fire of God is seen as so powerful and holy that it will kill all who come near in irreverence and unholiness. The fire is the same, yet it can either deliver or kill.

The fire of God is like nuclear power atop Mt. Sinai. This power can bring either life or death. If obedient, the fire of God will bring His very words to the people. These words, like the pillar of fire by night, will be "a lamp for my steps." If disobedient, the fire will explode in a holocaust to destroy and kill.

Today we face similar questions of obedience or disobedience. We can either turn to the fire of God and live, or we can turn to the fire of hell and die. One fire brings life, the other brings death. Both have the power of a huge volcano or nuclear holocaust. The power can be used either to save or destroy, to deliver or oppress. The fire is definitely coming. Of this there is no longer any question. It is, however, up to us to choose how it will be used.

119

9
Jesus: The Fire of Tabor and Apocalypse

Two important scriptural references to the fire of God directly relate to the person of Jesus. One is in the gospels during His transfiguration. The other is from the Apocalypse. Both speak of fire and light in a highly mystical way.

The transfiguration is an event in the life of Christ that hearkens directly back to the theophanies of fire in the Old Testament scriptures. It is meant, undoubtedly, to tie the authority of Jesus directly to the authority of both Moses and Elijah. Moses represents the Law and the theophanies of Horeb and Sinai, while Elijah represents the prophets and the powerful image of fire from heaven relating to his life and ministry. Jesus is seen here as fulfilling the glories of both by His transfiguration on Mt. Tabor.

The account from St. Matthew is as follows: "Jesus took Peter, James, and his brother John and led them up on a high mountain by themselves. He was transfigured before their eyes. His face became as dazzling as the sun, his clothes as radiant as light. Suddenly Moses and Elijah appeared to them conversing with him. . . . Suddenly a bright cloud overshadowed them. Out of the cloud came a voice which said: 'This is my beloved Son on whom my favor rests. Listen to him.' When they heard that the disciples fell forward on the ground, overcome with fear. Jesus came toward them and laying his hand on them, said, 'Get up! Do not be afraid.' When they looked up they did not see anyone but Jesus."

The similarities with the fire theophanies of Moses are most striking. Like Moses, only a select group go up the high mountain. Like Moses, they enter into a bright cloud of fire. Like Moses, the disciples are overcome with fear until assured that they will not die from such an immediate encounter with the fire or light of God. Especially significant is the actual transfiguration of Christ.

"His face became dazzling as the sun, his clothes radiant as light." This harkens back directly to Moses' intimacy with God. When Moses went up the mountain of God, he "stayed there with the Lord forty days and forty nights, without eating any food or drinking any water, and he wrote on the tablets the words of the covenant, the ten commandments. As Moses came down from Mt. Sinai with the two tablets of the commandments in his hands, he did not know that the skin of his face had become radiant while he conversed with the Lord. When Aaron, then, and the other Israelites saw Moses and noticed how radiant the skin of his face had become, they were afraid to come near him. Only after Moses called to them did Aaron and all the rulers of the community come back to him." Notice here the striking similarity between the response of those close to Jesus and Moses!

The conclusion from the similarities is clear: Jesus is a second Moses. As Moses was the lawgiver for the Old Covenant, Jesus is the lawgiver for the New Covenant. As Moses delivers the people of Israel, Jesus delivers all the world!

There is another similarity in the transfiguration. It is to the prophets! This is symbolized in the presence of Elijah. Elijah, too, was a man of God's fire. Elijah spoke out boldly against the prophets of the god Baal. Though in a minority, he spoke out boldly against the tendency of the majority to compromise with the philosophies and religions of the world. He challenged the people to choose between God and the gods of the secular world. He said to the people, "How long will you straddle the issue? If the Lord is God, follow him; if Baal, follow him."

Accused of being a troublemaker by the authorities, Elijah responds: "It is not I who disturb Israel, but you and your family, by forsaking the commands of the Lord and following the Baals." This, of course, led to Elijah's famous confrontation with the prophets of Baal on Mt. Carmel, where "the Lord's fire came down and consumed the holocaust" Elijah had prepared. "At seeing this, all the people fell prostrate and said 'The Lord is God! The Lord is God!'"

122

Do we compromise the purity of our faith with the philosophies and religions of the world? Are we willing to stand up against the majority when the majority is not following the true God? This is the fire of Elijah. This is the awesome fire of God that not only consumed the holocaust on Mt. Carmel but finally took Elijah up into heaven without tasting death! Does this fire take our spirits into heaven "in a whirlwind" even while we remain on earth?

There is also a similarity to the prophet Daniel. He, too, speaks of one whose clothing is radiant as light, but with Daniel this is a direct reference to God. "Thrones were set up and the Ancient One took his throne. His clothing was snow bright, and the hair on his head as white as wool; His throne was flames of fire with wheels of burning fire." This fire, of course, reminds us of the fire of God involved with the call of the prophet Ezekiel. But more importantly it emphasizes the divine dimension of the images and symbols used in the account of Jesus' transfiguration.

The transfiguration, therefore, brings out Jesus' identity not only with Moses but also with God. He is not only the prophet of the law; He is the giver of the law. He is not only lawgiver and prophet; Jesus is God! The symbols of the transfiguration emphasize this awesome mystery: Jesus is both God and man.

For the Orthodox Christians of the East, the fire and transfiguring light of Tabor is not something to be experienced only by Moses, or the prophets, or even Jesus Christ. It is to be experienced by all. As we come to share in the divine life of Jesus more and more we, too, will come to taste of the divinity of Christ, even as He first shared in our humanity. We come to be called Christians, or "like Christ," so we come to share even in the mystical and transfiguring light of Tabor.

Only after we have been deified by Christ in our life can we come to gaze upon the constant and eternal Taboric Light without fear. Only now that the Divine has taken on flesh can flesh look upon the Divine. What once brought fear and terror now brings comfort and unsurpassable joy. What once symbolized the glory of the Transcendant is now manifested in the humility of the Incarnate One. Unworthy though we are, we now share in this spiritual glory, because He first shared in our humble flesh.

St. Francis is said to have actually had an experience similar to the transfiguration, for the saint was an almost perfect follower of Christ. In the *Little Flowers* we read "St. Francis went out to a hill near the Place [a poor hermitage of the brothers] where there was a very beautiful forest in order to pray alone in a small hut that was there. . . . [A witness saw] a marvelous light completely surrounding St. Francis, and in that light he saw Christ and the Blessed Virgin Mary and St. John the Baptist and St. John the Evangelist and a great throng of angels, who were talking with St. Francis."

It is significant that a similar light of divine fire was seen about St. Francis so that he is seen as a type of Elijah for his era. It seems that when Francis was separated from his Brothers while away on a preaching mission, "about midnight a fiery chariot of extraordinary brilliance came in the door of the hut and turned here and there three times about the room. It was surmounted by a globe of light which looked like the sun and lit up the darkness. Those who were awake were dumbfounded, while the others woke up terrified; they could feel the light penetrating their hearts . . . and their consciences were laid bare to one another by force of its brightness. . . . They all realized simultaneously that their father [Francis] who was absent from them in person was present with them in spirit under the appearance of the vision. They were sure God had shown him to them in this glorious chariot of fire, radiant with the splendor of heaven and inflamed with burning ardor, so that they might follow him as loyal disciples." Like a second Elijah, God had made Francis a "chariot and charioteer" for all spiritual people. Certainly, it seems that God opened the eyes of these ordinary men at the request of St. Francis, so that they might contemplate His divine power, just as He had once opened the eyes of the servant of the prophet Elias, so that he could see "the whole mountainside beset with flaming horses and chariots there about Elias."

I myself had an experience of seeing Jesus in such a light in a vision. Whether or not I saw this light of Jesus with my physical eyes, I honestly do not know. I know I looked with my eyes, and my mind perceived Jesus in glorious light. God created me with a human psychology so I suppose He can use that human psychology to reach me with His divine light if He wants to. All I know is that this vision changed my life and ignited in me a fire of God that lights up my whole soul! St. Paul similarly speaks of a vision: "Whether he was in or outside his body I cannot say, only God can say—a man who was snatched up to third heaven. I know that this man— whether in or outside his body I do not know, God knows—was snatched up to Paradise to hear words which cannot be uttered."

Such mystical experiences are definitely possible for those who follow Christ. They are not beyond the realm of our spiritual experience on earth. We are "already seated with Christ" even while here on earth, says St. Paul. These experiences are simply a matter of the supernatural breaking through into and transforming the natural. Even as Christ was incarnated into the world to manifest the glory of the divine among and through the human, so now can those who follow Christ share in His divine glory even while following the footsteps of His humility and humanity.

Such gifts of visions should not necessarily be sought, but they should not be rejected either. St. Paul says, "Set your hearts on spiritual gifts," but he never mentions seeking after actual visions or revelations. He does, however, mention prophecy, miracles, and tongues, so the principle of seeking extraordinary gifts from God is encouraged by Paul as long as they increase the flame of love. He might say, "Set your hearts on spiritual gifts," but he first says, "Seek eagerly after love." He might give many rules that cautiously permit the exercising of spiritual gifts, but his most beautiful and inspired words are on love.

Boniface Maes, in his book *Franciscan Mysticism*, enthusiastically describes the experience of the extraordinary gifts of God, but he also concludes: "Be most careful, then, to avoid giving access to your heart to any curious desire for spiritual gifts, experimental or sensible sweetness, revelations, etc., lest the Angel of shadows, finding in this curiosity and self-seeking an open field for his operations, transform himself into an Angel of light for your deception. May, then, a devout soul never desire these things or them of God? To this I reply: one may do so in so far as it seems to us that by them our heart will be more inflamed with love for God."

St. John seems to have experienced such a revelation of Christ. He says, "On the Lord's day I was caught up in ecstasy, and I heard behind me a piercing voice like the sound of a trumpet.... I turned around to see whose voice it was that spoke to me. When I did so I saw seven lampstands of gold, and among the lampstands One like the Son of Man wearing an ankle-length robe, with a sash of gold about his breast. The hair of his head was white wool and his eyes blazed like fire. His feet gleamed like polished brass refined in a furnace, and his voice sounded like the roar of rushing waters. In his right hand he held seven stars. A sharp, two-edged sword came out of his mouth, and his face shone like the sun at its brightest."

This vision of Christ is bright with symbolism! It obviously alludes to many Old Testament images of God. The sound of His voice reminds us of the God of the Law atop Horeb and Sinai. The two-edged sword of His mouth reminds us of Elijah on Mt. Carmel against the prophets of Baal. His appearance is especially a direct reference to the prophetic book of Daniel. His radiant face recalls the transfiguration on Mt. Tabor. The image of fire is used throughout.

Here I would like to emphasize the line, "His eyes blazed like fire." Jesus says, "The eye is the body's lamp," and Proverbs has it, "A lamp from the Lord is the spirit of man." From this has grown the common saying, "The eyes are the window of the soul."

If Jesus' eyes are ablaze like fire, then His soul must be on fire! His soul is on fire because He reflects the perfect image of the Father's glory. His eyes reflect His soul, and His soul reflects the image of the Father. If we see a fire in Jesus' eyes it is because they are the perfect reflection of the image of the fire of God the Father.

St. Paul says of Jesus, "He is the image of the invisible God." The letter to the Hebrews continues, "This Son is the reflection of

126

the Father's glory, the exact representation of the Father's being."
St. Augustine explains the eternal begottenness of the Son from the
Father as follows: "Fire gives forth light: light flows out from fire.
No one doubts that the splendor derives from the fire, not the fire
from the splendor. Let us consider the fire as the Father, whence
proceeds this splendor. If there be no fire there is no splendor. As
soon as I light the fire, fire and light leap up together. Give me fire
without light, and I shall believe the Father was without the Son."

In this analogy St. Augustine considers the perceived fire of
Jesus as coming only from the fire of the Father. The analogy is an
explanation of the Son being called the image of the Father, and of
the eternal dimension of the Son's begotteness from the Father. If
the fire of the Father is eternal, then so must be the splendor of the
light it begets in the Son.

From this we can conclude that all of the Old Testament theophanies of fire are completely reflected and perfectly fulfilled in
the person of Jesus. The fire of the Father is not impersonal, it is
living in the person of the Father. What was once only alluded to
in the impersonal fire of nature is now revealed in the personal fire
of Jesus Christ. The fires of old that were limited to specific times
and places on earth are now fulfilled in the divine fire of Christ
who is with us always even unto the end of the world. As Hebrews
says, "In times past God spoke to our ancestors many times and in
many ways through the prophets, but in these last days he has spoken to us through His Son."

10
The Cross: The Fire of Stigmata

Perhaps the most powerful image the Christian can meditate on is the cross. The cross is the distinctive mark of honor for the Christian. Its humiliation is our glory, its poverty our wealth, its daily death to self our key to eternal life. It is the center of our entire life with God. It is the pivotal point of history, standing midway between our creation, fall, and our final redemption in glory. On the cross heaven and earth were reconciled. God and man embraced, and the things of time were reconciled with God's absolute being in eternity.

As to the all encompassing nature of the cross in the Christian life, St. Paul says, "May I never boast of anything but the cross of our Lord Jesus Christ! Through it, the world has been crucified to me and I to the world. . . . All that matters is that one is created anew." Paul sees the cross as a central experience to participating fully in the charismatic "fruit of the Spirit." He says, "The fruit of the Spirit is love, joy, peace, patient endurance, kindness, generosity, faith, mildness, and chastity. Against such there is no law! Those who belong to Christ Jesus have crucified their flesh with its passions and desires. Since we live by the Spirit, let us follow the Spirit's lead."

Paul experiences the cross of Jesus in a deeply personal way. For him it is not just a theological gymnastic to achieve reconciliation between God and humankind. It is an experience! It is embraced in a way that permeates his whole soul. It is a sword that, with Mary, pierces his heart. It is a fiery stigmata that, *with* St. Francis, he bears in his very body.

Of this Paul says, "Henceforth, let no man trouble me, for I bear the brand marks of Jesus in my own body." He says to the Colossians, "In my own flesh I fill up what is lacking in the sufferings of Christ for the sake of his body, the church." For St. Paul the cross is the guideline for his whole way of life. He says, "Peace and mercy on all who follow this rule of life." For Paul this "rule" is the greatest of all religious rules. It is greater than that of St. Augustine or St. Benedict. It is greater than that of St. Francis, even though Francis himself is the great bearer of the marks of Christ, the stigmata.

The cross is at once both practical and mystical. It can provide St. Paul, St. Augustine, St. Benedict, and St. Francis with an essential "rule" for life. It guides us daily on our journey to God, providing a constitution for situations both small and great. Yet in its spiritual essence it crosses over into the mystical in a way that both fulfills and defies the mind. It pierces the heart and melts the soul to its deepest center in a way that leaves us stammering or awestruck in silence in response to the word of God. All that is solid and rigid melts like wax before the flame of the love of God. It is then that we are once more pliable, easily reshaped and reformed according to the image of God.

This is the way the cross worked for St. Francis. It was like a mystical flame that pierced him and took up residence in his very soul. Bonaventure says of him, "The memory of Christ Jesus crucified was ever present in the depths of his heart like a bundle of myrrh, and he longed to be transformed into Him by the fire of love."

St. Bonaventure says that it is meditation upon the cross of Jesus Christ that, in fact, keeps the fire of God's love burning within our hearts. "Anyone who wishes to keep the flame of ardor alive within himself should frequently—or rather, incessantly—contemplate in his heart Christ dying upon the cross."

Earlier we said that an attitude of constant praise and thanksgiving was necessary to enter into the presence of God and to overcome sin. Here we see that it's also a constant meditation on the cross that stirs up the love of God within our souls. Notice that Bonaventure says "contemplate in his heart." It is not just a mental practice. The cross of Jesus Christ is a constant attitude that must permeate everything we are about. It becomes so much a part of us that we cannot be thought of without it. We and the cross become one. It transforms and reforms our personality and attitude according to the attitude and person of Jesus Christ.

As Paul says to the Philippians, "The attitude you should have is the one that Christ Jesus had: He always had the nature of God, but he did not think that by force he should try to become equal with God. Instead of this, of his own free will he gave up all he had, and took the nature of a servant. He became like man and appeared in human likeness. He was humble and walked the path of obedience all the way to death—the death on the cross. For this reason God raised him to the highest place above and gave him the name that is greater than any other name. And so, in honor of the name of Jesus, all beings in heaven, on earth, and in the world below will fall on their knees, and all will openly proclaim that Jesus Christ is Lord, to the glory of God the Father."

As St. Bonaventure says of St. Francis and the first friars, "Christ's cross was their book and they studied it day and night, at the exhortation and after the example of their father who never stopped talking to them about the cross."

For Francis, this was not just an intellectual experience. It was mystical. It permeated his soul. As Bonaventure says again, "His soul melted at the sight, and the memory of Christ's passion was impressed on the depths of his heart so vividly that whenever he thought of it, he could scarcely restrain his sights and tears. . . . He realized immediately that the words of the Gospel were addressed to him, 'If you have a mind to come my way, renounce yourself, and take up your cross and follow me'" (Matt. 16:24).

Bonaventure wrote to the Franciscan Sisters, "Your heart is the altar of God. It is here that the fire of intense love must burn always. You are to feed it every day with the wood of the cross of Christ and the commemoration of His passion. . . . Therefore, let your love lead your steps to Jesus wounded, to Jesus crowned with thorns, to Jesus fastened upon the gibbet of the cross. . . . Enter with your whole being through the door of His side into Jesus' heart itself. There, transformed into Christ by your burning love for the Crucified, pierced by the nails of the fear of God, wounded by the spear of superabounding love, transfixed by the sword of intimate compassion, seek nothing, desire nothing, wish for no consolation, other than to be able to die with Christ on the cross."

Here we are called not only to be wounded ourselves by Christ. We are called actually to enter Christ's heart through His wounds. Here we enter Him because He has first wounded us with the cross and entered us through the Spirit. He enters us and we enter Him. We become one even as a husband and wife become one in sexual union. That is why scripture uses the analogy of a bride and groom to best describe the intimate and deeply personal love relationship shared between Jesus and His Church and Jesus and individual souls.

Bonaventure quotes St. Bernard and St. Augustine to emphasize this, saying of Jesus' love for us on the cross, "Behold the head of Christ leaning down to kiss us, his arms stretched out for an embrace, his hands pierced for a gift of blood, his side opened for loving, his whole body extended for a complete spending of himself."

This whole experience is typified in the stigmata of St. Francis of Assisi. Bonaventure says, "The fire of divine love burned the more perfectly in his heart for all that it only became visible in his flesh later on in his life."

This description of the stigmata as a burning fire of love continues in Bonaventure's account. "Two years before his death, after a period of intense activity, he was led by Divine Providence to a high mountain called La Verna, where he could be alone. . . . He was all on fire with heavenly desires and he realized that the gifts of divine grace were being poured out over him in greater abundance than ever. . . . His body had already been weakened by the austerity of his past life and the fact that he had carried our Lord's Cross without interruption. . . . The unquenchable fire of love for Jesus in his goodness had become a blazing light of flame. . . . The fervor of his seraphic longing raised Francis up to God and, in an ecstasy of compassion, made him like Christ who allowed himself to be crucified in the excess of his love. Then one morning about the feast of the Exaltation of the Holy Cross, while he was praying on the mountainside, Francis saw a Seraph with fiery wings coming down from the highest point in the heavens. . . . Then he saw the image of a Man crucified in the midst of the wings, with his hands and feet stretched out and nailed to a cross. . . . Francis was dumbfounded at the sight and his heart was flooded with a mixture of joy and sorrow. . . . He was lost in wonder." After this experience, St. Francis discovered the marks of Jesus Christ imprinted in his hands his feet and his side! He became the first known stigmatist in Christian history.

The experience of stigmata is a mystical encounter with Christ that expands St. Francis's heart and mind. He experiences joy and sorrow all at once. It is as if Jesus pierced through Francis's earthly body and expanded his soul in both directions at once.

I have often said that all of us experience this interior expansion when we truly encounter Jesus Christ. If we were to see all of the potential glory or all of the existent sin in our lives all at once we would more than likely die. Usually God allows us to glimpse into these realities a bit at a time. He lets us see our sin only as we are able to overcome it by grace. He lets us see our glory in Christ only as we are humble enough to deal with it.

Then suddenly, after a period of preparation, God allows some souls to experience the fullness of the cross in one mystical encounter. In this mystical experience, oftentimes in an instant, oftentimes after hours, the soul intuitively is visited by the fullness of this grace, which is too much for the normal soul to contain. It is too much to comprehend. It is as if a divine fire explodes from the inside out through our entire soul. Divine nails come from heaven, piercing our earthly self and exploding in our deepest heart and soul. This, in turn, transforms our entire life. This divine fire may not directly imprint our flesh, but it will indelibly imprint our soul. Once our soul has been stigmatized by Christ, our external life must be transformed and changed into the image of the Crucified as well. Thus, it will permanently leave the marks of the cross on our soul. The marks will be eternal!

Rapture and Ecstasy

The gift of rapture or the experience of ecstasy often follow directly after the meditation on creation, scripture, or, in particular, after the meditation on the fire of the cross of Jesus Christ. The mind creatively visualizes and the heart is stirred. After the heart and spirit are stirred the soul experiences visitations from the Lover that are beyond human thought or words. The human spirit is "caught up" to heaven unexpectedly and enters into an ecstasy that so enlarges heart and mind that it extends beyond their meager human capacity. In both, the human capacities are enlarged and deified by a divine visitation that defies human capacity. The infinite is poured forth into the finite, so the human vessel feels it must surely burst. Yet, instead of bursting in destruction, it is made aware of its own human limitations and thus enabled to bear and be healed by the visit from the divine. Like a burning bush, the soul burns hot and bright in the visitation from God. Yet, instead of being destroyed, the soul is truly saved.

Bonaventure relates this experience to the Sisters: "Devotion may sometimes cause our spirit to 'lose hold of itself and rise above itself'; to pass into a state of rapture 'when we are inflamed with the ardor of such celestial desire that the whole world seems bitter and tiresome. The flame of intimate love, grown beyond human measure, makes the soul to swoon, to melt like wax, and to rise aloft like incense, higher and higher, to the very summit.' . . . Again, in rapture sometimes the grace occurs because of the height of admiration. 'When our soul is of contemplation' irradiated with divine light, and held in suspense by the wonder of supreme Beauty, it is thrown off its foundation. In the likeness of a flash of lightning, the deeper the soul is cast into the abyss by the contrast between Beauty and itself, the higher and faster does it rise to the sublime.' . . . Finally, rapture may come about through the height of Exultation. Our soul . . . completely forgets what it is and what it was, and its whole being becomes supernatural desire."

St. John of the Cross also speaks of this fire of rapture in direct connection to the stigmata of St. Francis of Assisi: "Cauterizing the soul by an intellectual form . . . it will feel that a seraphim is assailing it by means of an arrow or dart which is all afire with love. . . . And being wounded by this fiery dart, the soul feels the wound with unsurpassable delight. . . . The soul feels its ardor strengthen and increase and its love become so refined in this ardor that seemingly there are seas of loving fire within it, reaching to the heights and depths of the earthly and the heavenly spheres, imbuing all with love. It seems to it that the entire universe is a sea of love in which it is engulfed. . . . Few persons have reached these heights. . . . God sometimes permits an effect to extend to the bodily senses in the fashion in which it existed interiorly, the wound appears outwardly, as happened when the seraphim wounded St. Francis."

So it is with the fire of the cross. It is the height to which the flame of God's love can be fanned. As scripture says, "No greater love has any man than this, that he lay down his life for his friends." The cross is the highest expression of God's love for us. Likewise it is our highest expression of love for Him. There is no greater flame that can be fanned into existence. It burns the brightest, flares up the highest, and creates the hottest bed of coals that eventually heats the whole house of our lives.

The cross is the culmination of all meditation; it is the beginning of all purgation and illumination, and it is the consumation of our love union with God Himself. All that remains is to enter into the contemplative rest that follows the union of the full-fanned flames, where hot embers and slow-burning coals heat the entire house of God.

11
The Fire of Union and Contemplation

After the fires of purgation and illumination have been fanned into a full flame, hot-burning coals of contemplation are built up that give out a constant and steady heat to the house of our entire lives. It is necessary for roaring flames to be fanned up before the coals form in the fireplace, but the bright and high-reaching flames do not heat the house as effectively as the red-hot and steady-burning coals.

These coals represent the contemplative life. Once we have genuinely experienced the roaring flames of purgation from sin and illumination in divine love in our human lives, then we are ready for the hot embers of contemplation. In fact, these hot embers form quite naturally when the flames of purgation and illumination have genuinely burned bright in our life. If we faithfully and intentionally stoke and fan the fires of purgation and illumination through meditation, prayer, and praise, the coals of contemplation will be built up as a bed for the rest of our lives with seeming ease.

Many people, however, try to claim the experience of the burning coals of contemplation before they have really experienced the genuine fire of purgation and illumination. Never having really had the fire of purgation battle the fires of their own sins, never having had the fire of illumination rouse them to rapture and ecstasy after meditation on God's creation, God's scriptures, or the cross of Jesus Christ, never having really let the fire of God burn ardently in their very souls through the power of thanksgiving, praise, and mystical love, it is virtually impossible for them to build up a hot bed of coals that will burn slowly and steadily. Their fire will die and the house will grow ice-cold. Their only option will be to start all over again, building their fires from the broken pieces of kindling that are left of their lives. That is hard work, but even this will eventually succeed.

The Fire of God

There are many would-be contemplatives who have yet really to pass through the fire of purgation and illumination. They still live lives of immorality while considering themselves advanced contemplatives. Many look down their noses at the more emotional experiences of the charismatic. Neither of these attitudes is proper for the true contemplative.

Certainly, lives of immorality are not conducive to advanced contemplation. As John says, "If we say, 'We have fellowship with him,' while continuing to walk in darkness, we are liars and do not act in truth.... If we say, 'We are free of the guilt of sin,' we deceive ourselves.... If we say, 'We have never sinned,' we make him a liar and his word finds no place in us."

And as St. Paul says, concerning charismatic gifts, "Set your hearts on spiritual gifts," and, "I should like it if you all spoke in tongues," but, "make sure that everything is done properly and in order." Those who do not fully open themselves to the fire of purgation and illumination can never really enter fully into the fire of contemplation. They may think they are mature contemplatives, but they are deceiving themselves. They are not yet even beginners.

For those who have successfully built a bed of coals, it is easy to stoke their fires with the wood of the cross. The fires of purgation and illumination then become one with the coals of contemplation. One moves freely from the one to the other as a love relationship with Jesus Christ matures and daily becomes more balanced and peacefully integrated. A fire such as this can burn uninterrupted throughout an entire life of winter if faithfully tended from time to time.

This life will become a rhythm in the Spirit flowing from bright flames to hot coals and from hot coals back to burning flames. In the morning there will always be enough hot coals left from the night before to stoke up the flames of another roaring fire, and this roaring fire will build up yet another bed of steady-glowing embers of hot coals. Thus, day will flow into night and night into day, so that day after day the steady alternation between the fire of purgation and illumination and the coals of contemplation will bring balance and healthy integration into our full life with Jesus Christ.

The stages of progression are not mutually exclusive, however. Once you pass from one stage to another, you continue to experience the ones that have come before. Those who experience illumination continue to experience purgation, and the contemplative who experiences full union continues to experience both purgation and illumination. If anything, those who advance experience the preceding steps even more fully and intensely than before. Those who think they have moved on in a way exclusive of the preceding steps have actually yet to experience them fully. With true advancement all that has come before is enriched and completed. It all becomes one, yet it becomes even more defined. This, too, is a paradox and a mystery.

Bonaventure speaks of this progression as a "passing over" from meditation to pure contemplation. In meditation one still uses positive words and images to direct the mind and heart on the soul's journey to God. In contemplation one gives up words and images of God to simply "be" in God. It passes from the realms of the soul to the spirit, from the describable to the indescribable, from the knowable to the unknowable. One even passes from the emotional passion in rapturous and eccstatic union with Jesus to an experience of mystical union that transcends all human emotion. In this we become one with the divine.

As Bonaventure says, "Let us die, then, and pass over into the darkness; let us silence every care, every craving, every dream; with Christ crucified, let us pass 'out of this world to the Father'" (John 13:1).

Imageless Prayer

It is the experience of the cross of Jesus Christ that leads us to the imageless prayer of contemplation. In the cross, life-giving divinity is fully poured out in the ultimate and final experience of humanity —death. Divine fullness is poured out in emptiness. Pure existence is poured out in nothingness. Pure light is turned into darkness. He who knows all things cries out to the Father, "Why have you forsaken me?"

Here we find the absolute in mystery. We can touch the transcendent God only in the self-emptying of Jesus Christ the God-Man on the cross. We find the eternal God in a finite man in space and time, eternal life in a criminal's death. Here we can boldly state what we have come to absolutely know only with a feeble question. We can speak of a light only in terms of our own human blindness after having gazed into its divine brightness. We can state its fullness only in terms of emptiness and its knowability in terms of unknowing. This may seem like absolute nonsense and gibberish, but anyone who has experienced it knows it points to the wisdom of God.

Bonaventure says, "Negations seem to say less but actually they say more. Negative predications express transcendence. For instance, we say: God is not perceptible through the senses, but is above the senses; nor is He imaginable, intelligible, manifest, but is above all these concepts."

In his *Journey of the Mind to God* Bonaventure says, "Such a passing over as this is something mystical and very secret, and no one knows it except him who receives it, and no one receives it except him who desires it, and no one desires it unless the fire of the Holy Spirit, whom Christ sent to earth, inflames him to his very marrow."

Thus, the move into imageless contemplative prayer is a natural progression from the rapturous experience of charismatic prayer. The intentional stirring up of the Spirit through praise and thanksgiving in tongues and tears leads us to rapture and ecstasy. From rapture and ecstasy the soul moves very easily to the prayer of quiet and rests as on a Sabbath of imageless and wordless contemplation.

Bonaventure again uses the image of fire to relate the connectedness between the rapturous love of the cross and pure imageless contemplation. "If you wish to know how such things come about, consult grace, not doctrine; desire, not understanding; prayerful groaning, not studious reading; the Spouse, not the teacher; God, not man; darkness, not clarity. Consult, not light but the fire that completely inflames the mind and carries it over to God in transports of fervor and blazes of love. This fire is God. . . . Christ starts the flame with the fiery heat of his intense suffering. . . . Whoever loves this death may see God, for this is beyond doubt true: 'No man sees Me and still lives' (Exod. 33:20). Let us die, then, and pass over into the darkness."

Vladimir Lossky says of the seeming darkness of this intense light, "The divine light, being given in mystical experience, surpasses at the same time both sense and intellect. It is immaterial and is not apprehended by the senses; that is why St. Symeon, the New Theologian, while affirming its visibility yet calls it 'invisible fire.'"

It is not so much that God's light is darkness, for "God is light and in him there is no darkness at all." It is just that the light and fire are so intense that they seemingly leave one blinded. This blindness is at the same time a healing that restores our sight. This divine blindness heals us of our human blindness, and leaving us blinded, we find that we truly see. God is so intensely everywhere that it overwhelms us and He seems nowhere. He comes to us in His pure image, and we can describe him only as imageless.

St. Symeon says, "He comes with a certain image, but it is an image of God; for God could not appear under any image or figure; but he makes himself seem in his simplicity, formed in light without form, incomprehensible, ineffable. I can say no more. . . . We are completely unable to measure by our intellect, or express it in words."

Bonaventure speaks of the seeming darkness of the light of pure being: "When we face the very light of highest Being, not realizing that this supreme Darkness is actually the Light of our mind, we think we are not seeing anything. The same thing happens when our eyes gaze upon pure light: we think that we are not seeing anything."

He says of the pure Being, "It is the very first and the very last, it is the origin and final end of all things. Because it is eternal and all-present, surrounding and penetrating all duration, it is, as it were, both their center and their circumference. Because it is utterly simple and utterly great, it is wholly interior to all things and wholly exterior to them. 'It is intelligible sphere, the center of which is everywhere, and the circumference nowhere. 'Because it is supremely actual and immutable,' while remaining unmoved, it imparts motion to all. Because it is wholly perfect and wholly immeasurable, it is interior to all things, yet not enclosed; exterior to all things, yet not excluded above all things, yet not aloof; below all things, yet not their servant. . . . Even though all things are many and pure being is but one, it is 'all in all'" (1 Cor. 15:28).

Such knowledge is too great for the human intellect. It awes the mind and sends the heart into rapture. It lifts us to emotional fervor and then leaves us in total rest and contemplative peace. It takes us higher than we have ever dared look before, yet roots us more deeply in God than our previous knowledge about God was ever able to achieve. It expands us up and roots us down, so that the deeper we are rooted the higher we can climb. This happens in an intuitive flash of fire that leaves us so expanded in spirit that we think we will truly die in body so we might fully see the light of God! As Bonaventure concludes, "Nothing more is to come but the day of quiet, on which, in ecstatic intuition, the human mind rests after all its labors."

The Incarnation

Of course this same thing happens when we meditate on the incarnation of pure Being within Jesus. Here, that which is beyond imagining takes on flesh to lead us beyond all imagining. Heavenly image takes on the human image to transform the fallen human image back to the divine. This all occurs in the perfect image of Jesus.

Paul says, "He is the image of the invisible God. . . . It pleased God to make absolute fullness reside in him and by means of him, to reconcile everything in his person, both on earth and in the heavens, making peace through the blood of his cross." Likewise, the book of Hebrews says, "This Son is the reflection of the Father's glory, the exact representation of the Father's being."

This means that He who is beyond all form took on form to lead us all back to a glory that surpasses all possible description. "Eye has not seen, ear has not heard, nor has it so much as dawned on man what God has prepared for those who love Him." What God has in store for us has not even dawned upon our human mind! It is too glorious and too simple. No form can contain His divine image, no word can fully proclaim the living Word, no thought can perceive the fullness of the divine Idea.

Yet it is in Jesus that the indescribable takes on seemingly describable flesh. This, too, is a great mystery. We think we can describe the humanity of Jesus, yet we cannot. We think the transcendent God cannot be described, yet He gives us truths to be known in Christ. We know, yet we do not. We think we cannot, yet in Christ we can. In this mystery the imageless glory of divinity is reflected perfectly in the image of humanity. The infinite in the finite, the unknowable in the known, He who has always been shrouded by mysterious darkness in clear revelation of light. Yet, even this revelation itself constitutes a mystery that transports our souls from the knowability of pure contemplation in God.

As to the mysteries of the incarnation, Bonaventure also says, "In Him the First Principle is united with the last to be created; God is united with man formed on the sixth day; eternity is united with time-bound humanity, with a Man born of a Virgin in the fullness of ages; utter simplicity is united with the most composite, pure action with supreme passion and death, absolute perfection and immensity with lowliness, the supremely one and all-inclusive with an individual composite man, distinct from every other: the Man Jesus Christ. . . . This consideration brings about perfect enlightening of the mind, when the mind beholds man made, as on the sixth day, in the image of God. Since, therefore, an image is an express likeness, when our mind contemplates, in Christ the Son of God, our own humanity so wonderfully exalted and so ineffably present in Him; and when we thus behold in one and the same Being both the first and the last, the highest and the lowest, the circumference and the center, the Alpha and the Omega, the caused and the cause, the Creator and the creature . . . then our mind reaches a perfect object. Here, as on the sixth day, it reaches with God the perfection of enlightenment."

Thus, in contemplating the human image of Jesus, we will be led to the imageless and the divine. We will experience such an expansion of consciousness, that our mind will not be able to deal with the perfection of the reconciliation of opposites in this divine mystery. As we grasp it with our minds, it must by its nature jump, as it were, from the realm of the mind to the heart. It will then jump to the pure realm of spirit. Here, things are understood by intuition in a way that surpasses all understanding and all feeling. Here the unknowable is understood by unknowing, and the imageless is imagined beyond all images. Here, by moving beyond all images, we are reformed according to the image of Christ. Paradoxically, we can move beyond images only by meditating on Christ's image, and by contemplating the image of Christ we will move into the imageless realm of pure spirit. This happens perfectly only when contemplating the perfect coincidence of opposites reconciled with the image of the Jesus Christ, the Son of God and Son of Mary, fully human and fully divine. This harkens back to the revelation of God on Mt. Horeb: "The Lord spoke to you from the midst of the fire. You heard the sound of the words, but saw no form; there was only a voice."

Jesus is the full revelation of that voice. He is the word. He is the fire. He gives human form to the divine that surpasses all form.

144

We can look upon the form of Jesus if we desire to be led to the seeming formlessness of the divine. We can look upon the visible Jesus if we desire to be led to the fullness of the invisible. We can look upon Him who is the living Word if we desire to experience the profound silence of the transcendent God.

So it is the activity of Jesus in history that leads us to the perfect life of contemplation of the eternal. It is by listening to His word that we come into sacred silence. It is by gazing upon His simple and clear revelation that we are caught up into the mystery of the hidden. He is the door for the true contemplative. He is the fullness of all sacred mysteries. Those who come up some other way are destined to fail. Those who try another door will find themselves only in the outer rooms of the heavenly mansion. Jesus is the door that leads us to the inner chamber where the Lover waits to consummate intimately His union with His beloved. Those who come in another door remain outside. Intimacy is never fully experienced (John 10:1–18).

Jesus is the door that leads to the inner furnace of God's love where the glowing embers burn constantly, steadily, and hotly. These embers are the source of all other flames. They are the source of all heavenly fires throughout the face of all the earth. These embers give all heat and all comfort. They are the source of all light. They reveal the hidden and draw us back to this inner chamber of God's innermost heart.

These embers glow in the life of contemplation. They glow in the furnace of love that is the very heart of God. Jesus is the door of this fiery furnace. It is only through Him that we fully enter into the furnace actually to become one with the coals. If we abandon ourselves and lie naked upon this bed of coals, we will actually become one of the coals. Our body will burn and pass away, but our life will become a burning ember that will bring heat and comfort to all of the world.

It is as if we are costly frankincense put on the burning coal of God's love. The heat of God's ember will consume us. We will lose our particular form and actually become one with the coal. Yet as we become one with the coal, our lives will rise heavenward in a sweet-smelling smoky mist that will permeate everything on earth. We lose our form. We go up in smoke. We become nothing, yet we permeate everything. We burn on the bed of charcoal, yet the smell of our consummation is sweet and spreads through all the earth.

12
The Fire of Evangelization

If this fire of God brings light and warmth to our own souls, it will also bring light and warmth to others. A spiritual fire in our souls must be spread to others. Jesus said, "I have come to set a fire on the earth, how I wish it were ablaze already." This fire is not only for us, it is for others. Thus, the fire of purgation, illumination, and union also becomes a fire of evangelization.

For St. Francis this fire burned constantly. Bonaventure says, "Francis was all ablaze with fervid eagerness and he longed for the salvation of souls with heartfelt compassion.... All inflamed as he was with the fiery Spirit of Christ, he invited others to join him in the pursuit of perfect holiness, urging them to lead a life of penance. His words were full of the power of the Holy Spirit, never empty or ridiculous, and they went straight to the depths of the heart." Francis's words were like a blazing fire that penetrated the depths of the heart and filled the minds of his hearers with wonder. They had no claim of literary style but gave every sign of being the result of divine inspiration.

Of course, Jesus Himself commissions the apostles and all His followers to evangelize when He says, "Go, therefore, and make disciples of all the nations." The gospel according to St. Luke links this evangelization to the fire of the Holy Spirit. In it Jesus says, "In his name [the Messiah's], penance for the remission of sins is to be preached to all the nations, beginning at Jerusalem.... Remain here in the city until you are clothed with power from on high." In the Lucan tradition, the Acts of the Apostles also says, "You will receive power when the Holy Spirit comes down on you; then you will be my witnesses in Jerusalem, throughout Judea and Samaria, yes, even to the ends of the earth.... Wait for the fulfillment of my Father's promise, of which you have heard me speak. John baptized with water, but within a few days you will be baptized with the Holy Spirit." This baptism of the Spirit is a baptism of fire that consumes a person's whole soul in divine love for everyone and all.

Catholic Evangelization

I would like to address for a moment some remarks on evangelization specifically to my fellow Roman Catholics. I am a convert to Catholicism and am grateful that I have been able to bring to it some enriching experiences and learnings from my Protestant past, but I believe the Catholic Church holds extraordinary potential for the future of our world. Today, the Catholic Church is like a sleeping giant. But when it comes to evangelization, it very much needs some of the ardor of its Protestant brothers and sisters in spreading its fire of faith. It is time for the sleeper to awaken!

It is also time for Catholics to begin to mobilize and shout the good news of Jesus Christ from the housetops! We Catholics have been ashamed of our past for too long. We are no longer the Church we were a hundred years ago, or even thirty years ago. It is time to emphasize what we *are* rather than what we *were*. Mistakes from our past will be forgiven by God, but if we do not share our fire with others, the world will grow cold and dark and could even die. We must emphasize what we are and look to evangelize the world for the future.

Never before has it been so exciting to be a Catholic and a Christian, but it is time for the Catholic Christian people of the West to show enthusiasm for their faith in Jesus Christ and share it with all the world! We Catholics have answers the world is looking for. We have the Bread of Life, which every human heart hungers for. We have the gospel of Jesus Christ, which speaks to every area of life, every arena of challenge, in a way that is uncompromising and life-giving. There is no group of charismatics as united as the members of the Catholic charismatic renewal. There is no con-

148

templative or mystical tradition so rich and balanced as the mystical tradition of our faith. There is no pro-life movement more powerful. There is no peace and social-justice movement so balanced, active and so effective. No other Christian evangelist can proclaim the gospel of Jesus Christ with such profound effect as the pope. Even Billy Graham, an inspiration around the world, never spoke to so many at his crusades, nor has Pat Robertson ever reached so many with his television coverage. Large numbers of Protestants as well as Catholics see the pope as the foremost voice proclaiming the gospel of Jesus Christ, uncompromisingly and clearly throughout the world.

I ask Catholics to remember that we have stood, since the beginning, for life in the face of legalized death. We have stood around the world for basic human rights in the face of unjust governments. We have stood for peace in the face of a nuclear holocaust. We have stood for a just and equal distribution of the world's wealth in the face of the rampant materialism of the West, and for freedom of religion in the face of the atheism of the Communists. Actually, the words Catholic and ecumenical are not exclusive but inclusive; to be uncompromisingly Catholic is to assure respect and liberty for every other religion of the world. Be it to governments, cultures, or individual human hearts, the Catholic Church has proclaimed the freedom and the good news of Jesus Christ to the entire world. With renewed enthusiasm, and in cooperation with other religious bodies, it can do even more!

I say again: It is time to mobilize! This mobilization of the Catholic, Christian Body of Christ, in harmony with its Protestant brethren, is potentially awesome. Its ramifications are vast. Can you imagine such a large body of people standing uncompromisingly for the peace that comes through the nonresistance taught by the gospel of Jesus Christ? Can you imagine so many people radically changing their materialistic life-styles to share with the poor of this world? Can you imagine so many people actively changing from the lust of sin to righteousness, from anger to love, from gossip and slander to constant words of edification and thanks?

Can you imagine an army of prayer-warriors that dips into the full Catholic tradition of contemplative and charismatic prayer? I honestly do not know where such a spiritual revolution would lead. I know it could change entire nations and would certainly radically change our materialistic American culture. It would change the very fabric of our society today and build a better future for tomorrow.

Who knows—it might even bring an entire new form of God's just government on the face of the earth, one the world has never seen before. This is precisely what happened with the Founding Fathers of the United States. Who is to say it could not happen again? Who is to say God doesn't have yet a better form of government to give to protect the basic human rights of the people He created and loves? Perhaps it is time for just such an exciting and radical leap into Godly idealism once more. It takes faith. It means great risk. But in Christ Jesus such a risk pays off. It brings a spiritual revolution—a resurrection that far surpasses our wildest dreams.

This revolution, however, is not primarily political but rather spiritual. It is not built on politics, but on Jesus. It is not established by military power, but by the power of the Holy Spirit.

But as the spiritual world affects the material, so will our spiritual revolution affect the political realm. While the spiritual emphasis remains primary, the political will not necessarily be excluded. As John Henry Newman said, the Church, by its nature, must grow to influence authoritatively both the spiritual and political arenas of the country in which it is found. It affects both the faith and the morality of a nation. If it only affected their faith the political arena would never be involved in this revolution. But since the morality of a people is included, the Church immediately becomes a force of both spiritual and political revolution when a given government and its people are both faithless and immoral. This is true especially when considering the morality or immorality of laws in some countries concerning basic human rights. Of course, the use of physical violence is not proper in a truly Christian revolution. I am not at all suggesting, advocating, or supporting a spiritual revolution achieved by violence and for the peace of Jesus Christ.

The Adventure of Following Christ

In speaking of our future in heaven, St. John says, "Dearly beloved, we are God's children now; what we shall later be has not yet come to light." This principle also applies in part to the future of this present age. As we grow into the future in Christ we are constantly made new. The old passes away. We are constantly on an adventure into the unknown! Living our lives as followers of Jesus Christ, we must constantly and consistently apply His love and His teachings to the new set of circumstances we always face. This means the changeless gospel of Jesus Christ is constantly growing and taking on new forms as we meet the challenges of our constantly changing world. The gospel is our rock in this world, but it is not static. It is continuously made new by the power of the Holy Spirit and by the way we manifest it in the constantly changing circumstances of this world. The gospel lives, it develops, and grows. It builds in an ever-unfolding continuity upon what it was and into what it is not yet. Jesus said, "The man who has faith in me will do the works I do, and greater far than these." We will do even greater things than Jesus if we really have faith in Jesus. His power grows!

This means that as we face greater challenges, Jesus will work greater miracles. As we face more specific questions, Jesus will give us more specific answers. We will not contradict what has come before, but we will build upon it. If we refuse to build up higher the ramparts of the city of God, we will stand still and die. We will stop growing.

Evangelization is, after all, just a matter of growing. A tree spreads its roots and its branches into new space as it grows older. Likewise, as the Church grows older in time, it must stretch out its roots and branches into new space. Otherwise it is not growing. Just as a tree dies when it stops growing, so will the Church die if and when it stops stretching out to bring the gospel of Jesus Christ into new time and space throughout all creation.

Evangelization Programs

There are, of course, many expressions of evangelization, but the most important expression is simply the Christian life itself. Jesus says, "The gift you have received, give as a gift." If you have received the gift, or grace, of Jesus into your life you cannot help but share it. If, however, you have not personally received Jesus into your life, no matter how hard you try to evangelize you cannot.

Almost every church has an evangelization program. Most of these programs are good in themselves. But if the people within these programs do not have a relationship with Jesus, they cannot share that relationship effectively with others. You cannot evangelize until you have been evangelized. You cannot share what you do not have. You cannot give away what you do not possess.

If your evangelization programs are not working, perhaps it is not the program that is weak. It might be the people behind the program! Programs are unsuccessful without successful people. Programs do not save people, Jesus does! If your evangelization programs are not working, first make sure the people behind the programs are evangelized. Then almost any valid program will succeed.

It is similar to using prepared childbirth programs with married couples. These programs can obviously be very helpful with couples if the woman is pregnant. But the programs for prepared childbirth are useless if the woman is not pregnant! You can go through program after program, but if you are not pregnant, you won't have a baby. Conversely, if you are impregnated, you will have a baby with or without a prepared childbirth program. The program makes things easier during childbirth, but the program is useless if the woman is not pregnant.

So it is with evangelization programs. If you have first been evangelized by Jesus Christ, evangelization is a very natural process. Programs can be helpful, but even without a program the bride impregnated by Jesus Christ will give birth to children bearing His name and image. Programs without spiritually impregnated people are pointless. But evangelization programs made up of people who have first been evangelized by Jesus Christ are almost sure to succeed.

Sometimes, however, evangelization programs bring people together. And when Christian people come together they strengthen one another. In this sense evangelization programs themselves can actually evangelize the evangelizers. More often than not, when I go out to minister, I am the one who is ministered to. When I sing to a shut-in, she, not I, is the apostle. When I preach to a crowd, they energize me. When I go out in team ministry, it is my brother who ministers to me so that I might minister to others. I, likewise, do the same for him.

An Evangelization Program for Catholics and Protestants Alike

There is, therefore, a specific program I would like to share with my fellow Catholics, and remind my Protestant friends about its usefulness. It is the door-to-door ministry of evangelization. For years my Protestant brothers and sisters have successfully engaged in such a ministry, yet certain variations of their approach have turned many people off. Because of that, Catholics have been hesitant to share the good news of Jesus Christ in this way.

The door-to-door ministry I am engaged in is a ministry program of presence. We do not *necessarily* go out with tracts or prepared Bible quotes. We do not have a set of confronting questions. We do not even go out to take a parish census. All we do is go out to care. We knock on doors to share the care and concern of Jesus Christ with the people behind the doors. We do not look at them as prospective converts. We look at them as real people with living souls.

In this ministry we knock on doors only to say that we are Catholic Christians and that we care. We don't try to get them into a particular church or get them to come to a church program. We ask them only if there is anything they would like us to pray for.

We don't push praying with them on the spot. We offer to pray for them when we return to a church.

Usually people respond to us by saying they are not Catholic. In our area the population is only 2 percent Catholic. Most church-goers here are Baptist, Methodist, or interdenominational. Sometimes they say they are not Christian at all. We assure them that's all right. God loves all people right where they are, and so do we. We assure them that we aren't trying to "convert" them to our particular Church. As soon as they realize we have no hidden agenda, they usually open up. They share freely about the mother or father who is in the nursing home, the husband or wife they are having difficulty with, or the son or daughter who is straying from a good Christian or moral life. Often we will spend a fair amount of time in each home, just listening and reassuring them of our concern. Then the fact that we are Catholic Christians speaks more loudly than many words. A few words suffice and speak with the power of God's love.

In this ministry we work with the existing local churches. We do not proselytize, we evangelize! This means we encourage people to attend their own denominational church as long as they at least hear about Jesus and God. We let any interest they might have in Catholicism truly be a work of the Spirit. If they are interested they will ask. If they ask we will freely answer. In this way many come to convert first to Jesus Christ and then to Catholicism. I assume this principle would work equally well for Baptist door-to-door programs, or Lutheran, or Methodist, or Presbyterian, or any Christian denomination. We do not seek to convert them to a church. We convert them to Jesus and let Jesus lead them to his Church.

Another thing about this ministry is its poverty. We do not go out with the "wealth" of a preprepared pitch. We go out only to love and care for the people we meet with the love Jesus Christ has given us.

This love is vulnerable. It is poor. It is also a risk. It is a scary thing to approach someone's door with very little actually to say to the person or persons inside. All we say is, "Hello, we're the Franciscan Brothers from the Catholic parish. We're in the neighborhood saying hello, and seeing if there is anything you would like us to

154

pray for." That's all the security we have! After that the whole encounter is a risk. They could tell us they hate Catholics. They could call the cops. Likewise, they could totally unburden their souls. They could offer the welfare of their eternal souls into our hands. All of these things are fightening. It is risky to meet the myriad of possible greetings with a simple greeting of Christ's peace.

Visibility

Another good thing about this ministry is its visibility. For too long Catholic Christians have walked around with their tails tucked between their legs for being Catholic! We have a wealth no other Christian church fully possesses. Our tradition is older and more sure. Our teachings are more balanced and time tested. We speak to a broad spectrum of human existence and contemporary issues from a base of solid and time-tested tradition.

The Catholic Church has been placed at this time in history for a specific reason. This is our time. It is our hour. It is time to use and proclaim the gospel of Jesus Christ without compromise. The Catholic faith has answers for the problems that face the world today. We alone have brought the gospel of Jesus Christ to his world for the last two thousand years in an unbroken historical continuity. We bring it to this point of history in a way that is developed, balanced and true. Yet we bring in a way that is radical and challenging!

In all humility and with fear and trembling I must say that no other church can claim such a wide-spread and complete fulfillment of the great commission of Jesus Christ. No other institution, secular or sacred, can claim such a wide spread humanitarian concern for basic human rights. No other organization has stood so long for so much with so little recognition or appreciation from other churches or the world at large.

It is time to be visible, to share the good news of Christ. Just because we have done so much in the past is no excuse to stop now. The challenges that face the world are immense. The darkness is widespread and threatens to expand. It is time to hold our lamps high. It is time to take the light of God into the very heart of the darkness. The lamp is the word of God. The light is the gospel of Jesus Christ.

We must immerse ourselves into the very fire of God so our whole lives might become a flame to take to others. Unless our souls are on fire we cannot be a light for others. Unless we become a hot burning ember for God, we cannot become a source from which the fire of God can spread to others. Immerse yourself in God's flame. Let Him burn away all the wood and the hay and the stubble of your life. Then you will become a precious stone in the kingdom of God, you will provide a home for the homeless. You will be like fire-tried metal to become God's armor for the defenseless and the poor. You will be a sword of truth for the misguided and a flame of love for the unloved and abandoned. If the fire of God burns in your own life, then you will be able to bring His fire to others.

Do your evangelization programs fail or do they succeed? Do you profess faith in Jesus Christ but never really share His love with others? If you are not evangelizing it is because you have not been evangelized. If you are not able to share Jesus Christ with others, then allow Jesus to share His life more completely with you. As St. James says, "What good is it to profess faith without practicing it?" If our lives manifest the faith we profess, our lives become a tool for evangelization.

No program will work without Christ. No evangelization crusade will succeed without the Evangelizer. But once you have been truly evangelized by Jesus Christ, you will become a powerful part of the ongoing evangelization of the Body of Christ. You will become a hot burning ember within the largest, the oldest, and the longest burning fireplace in the history of the whole world. You will become an active member of the fireplace that brings heat to the coldest corners of the world. You will evangelize because your own soul has been evangelized. You will bring heat to a cold world because your own soul is on fire. You will proclaim good news to a bad-news world, because you know God's love and God's truth through and through.

Evangelizing the Catholic Church

I do not want it to appear as if I think the Catholic Church, and only the Catholic Church, can be effective in spreading the gospel of Jesus Christ. The Church has many shortcomings, and while I believe she has been infallibly kept by God in her basic mission to impart truth in areas of faith and morality, she has often sinned in the actions of her humanity. If anything, the miracle is that Jesus still moves so powerfully through such a weak and sinful Church. We Catholics have much to be proud of, but we also have many sins to confess.

This means that the Catholic Church herself is a great place for Catholics to begin evangelizing! We have many "baptized pagans" who fill our church pews weekly. We might be the largest Church in the world (some 800 million), but how many of our members really know and experience the good news of a personal love relationship with Jesus Christ? Of course, there is an element of faith active within the soul of a person who weekly makes the commitment to come to church, hear the word of God, and receive the sacraments, but how many actively experience a saving faith in Jesus Christ daily?

These are questions we cannot adequately answer while here on earth. Only God can effectively judge a human soul. If a person professes faith in Christ, lives a basic moral life of penance or conversion, and willfully chooses to come forward to receive Jesus in Communion, who are we to turn him or her away.

What we must do is get the people who fill the church pews personally to enter into a love relationship with Jesus Christ. The word of God in the scriptures, and in particular the gospels, are proclaimed at every liturgy. The liturgy itself is filled with the gospel of Jesus Christ as it has been faithfully experienced, lived, and worshiped for two thousand years. All of the essentials of Jesus' good news are proclaimed and heard Sunday after Sunday. Songs of praise are sung and beautiful prayers are raised to God's highest heaven! Even if the music is spiritless and the homily without vigor, all is not in vain. Jesus always shows up personally in the Eucharist.

157

We may not have a good music group or a charismatic preacher, but Jesus still shows up!

But how do we get people to enter into a personal love relationship with Jesus? Even if our doctrine is correct and true, that is no guarantee. Even if our preaching and our music are impressive, there is no guarantee that someone's conversion is anything more than just an emotional trip.

People often ask me at my workshops for church musicians, "How do we get our people to pray?" My answer is simply, "Pray yourself." If you want those around you to enter into a personal love relationship with Jesus Christ, enter into one yourself. If you want people to worship Jesus prayerfully during the celebration of the divine liturgy, pray and worship yourself. Again, if you want to evangelize others, you must first be evangelized yourself by Jesus Christ. If this really happens in your life, evangelization cannot be stopped. You will begin evangelizing every place you go, even at church! Your smile will evangelize. Your countenance will evangelize. Your every word, secular or sacred, will spread the good news.

Whether you are a Catholic or a Protestant Christian, if your soul is truly set on fire by God, you will spread that fire to every dry branch, leaf, or twig you touch. True, some people are not yet "dry," they are not yet ready. But there are far more out there ready to receive the gospel than you might think! Jesus says, "The harvest is rich, but few are the workers." If you allow yourself to be evangelized, set on fire with God, you will begin spreading that fire to everyone you meet. Remember, Jesus says, "I have come to set a fire on the earth, how I wish it were ablaze already." Become a co-worker with Christ. Help Him set a fire. It is a fire that does not destroy. It is a fire that brings warmth and light. It is a fire that saves. It is the very fire of God!